TEACHING STRESS MANAGEMENT AND RELAXATION SKILLS: AN INSTRUCTOR'S GUIDE

John D. Curtis, Ph.D.
Richard A. Detert, Ph.D.
Jay Schindler, Ph.D.
Kip Zirkel, Ph.D.

Coulee Press
La Crosse, Wisconsin

International Standard Book Number 0-9611456-2-5

Manufactured in the United States of America

Coulee Press
P.O. Box 1744, La Crosse, Wisconsin 54602-1744

DEDICATION

To Dr. Beata Jencks, friend, teacher and
professional. We've enjoyed sharing the
knowledge you so willingly shared with us.

CONTENTS

FOREWORD

Any professional person interested in relieving clients of stress can read no more than a few paragraphs of *Teaching Stress Management and Relaxation Skills: An Instructor's Guide* before recognizing that this book is more than a description of various techniques for allaying stress. The authors, in a meticulous yet succinct manner, discuss the myriad factors that spell victory or defeat in a facilitator's effort to bring relaxation and serenity to all of his or her clients.

It is obvious from the time you open the book that the authors possess an encyclopedic knowledge in the area of stress management. Their attention to small but important details is reflected throughout the monograph. I know of no other manual of instruction for relaxation facilitators that concerns itself with such details as pitch, timbre and tone of the facilitator's voice, choice of vocabulary in communicating with clients, and methods of touching and feeling the extremities of clients.

I can think of no other book attempting to inform relaxation facilitators that approaches the merit of *Teaching Stress Management and Relaxation Skills: An Instructor's Guide* which you now hold in your hands. I urge you to proceed quickly to the first chapter. Long before you have reached the end of the book, you, too, will be impressed with its caliber of scholarly excellence.

Meyer Friedman, M.D.
Author of *TYPE A BEHAVIOR AND YOUR HEART*

Introduction

Teaching Stress Management and Relaxation Skills: An Instructor's Guide is a result of the authors' collective experience of over 35 years of teaching stress management, relaxation skills, and biofeedback. In addition, we've drawn from the experience of other facilitators; we've tested their suggestions in our classes and included their input, comments and suggestions where appropriate.

Throughout the book we've attempted to present tested suggestions and ideas in the most practical manner possible. You will note that we've broken from tradition and included Instructional Pointers not at the end of chapters but throughout the book where they make the most sense for the facilitator of a stress management or relaxation program. We've also used the term facilitator to represent the teacher, psychologist, nurse or other professional instructing the class or teaching the skills one-to-one. Whenever possible we've used the term client to represent the recipient of the information either individually or collectively in a class.

We hope you enjoy the book as much as we've enjoyed teaching our basic stress management classes and our teaching stress management classes. The enjoyment clients experience in a well conducted course makes the effort well worthwhile.

The following caution should be kept in mind. The information presented in this book is designed to supplement the background of a trained allied health professional who knows the limits of their own knowledge and experiences. It is *not* designed as the only background information needed. A professional person can see related concepts, draw relationships, solve problems and, thus, adapt this information to fit the situation appropriately.

We would like to thank a variety of people who have contributed to the success of this book. Thank you to our many students over the years who challenged us to keep abreast of current knowledge in the area of stress management. Without the help and suggestions of Mary Abel, Captain Harold Moe, Claire Rood, Judith McCaslin, Dr. Phillip Esten, Margaret Larson and Dr. Roger Grant this book would never have materialized. And, last and most important, we thank our wives and children for support and understanding while we spent time away from the families to accomplish our goal.

CHAPTER 1

THE ENVIRONMENT FOR
RELAXATION TRAINING

As a facilitator of a relaxation class, you will generally be responsible for selecting a site for your class. This chapter examines factors to consider during site selection in order to maximize your opportunity for success.

The chapter is divided into the following sections: room selection, lighting, and noise. Each section is followed by instructional pointers. These pointers help clarify and offer additional suggestions for each of the topics including ways to modify the environment.

ROOM SELECTION

Room selection and room modification are important factors in determining the success of a relaxation class. Few facilitators have the luxury of a room designed specifically for relaxation training. Therefore it is important that you not only select the best room possible but also recognize how to modify an existing room to make it more compatible with your class goals and objectives.

The room should include as many of the following factors as possible:

QUIET

If clients are just beginning relaxation training, a quiet room is one of the most important considerations in room selection. This will be discussed in more detail under the section entitled Noise.

CARPETING

Carpeted rooms are recommended for relaxation classes for the following reasons.

1. Carpeting suggests a more personal, relaxed setting such as a living room or a family room. A tiled or linoleum floor suggests a more impersonal, institutionalized room.

2. Carpeting reduces the noise level of the room. When someone moves a chair or drops an object, the carpet muffles the noise, thus reducing interference with relaxation.

3. Carpeting provides warmth. Cold floors can hinder relaxation while carpeting can facilitate it. Carpet also provides warmth in the minds of the clients.

4. Carpeting softens the floor. Clients often find it beneficial to lie on the floor to try maximum support positions. Without carpeting, many clients quickly notice the hardness of the floor which reduces the focus of attention on the relaxation techniques and increases attention on the uncomfortable feeling associated with the hardness. Many clients continually adjust positions as the technique progresses and are unable to achieve deep relaxation. Although carpeting may not entirely prevent this, it does make the floor a more comfortable place, one in which it is generally easier to relax.

ROOM SIZE

The size of the room also contributes to the success of a relaxation class.

1. If a room is too small, overcrowding results. Overcrowding leads to distractions and difficulty in learning how to relax.

2. If a room is too large, proper voice control is severely reduced or lost entirely. This, too, can hinder the effectiveness of many relaxation techniques.

To prevent room size from hindering your efforts, determine the number of clients in the class prior to selecting the room.

ATTRACTIVENESS

Rooms should be clean and colorful, while avoiding extremes in color. Relaxing pictures, posters, and furnishings can add to the relaxed atmosphere of a room. Overly bright colors, too many colors, and/or clutter do not provide a relaxed atmosphere. Common sense seems to be the best criterion for keeping the room attractive and relaxing.

WINDOWS AND DOORS

Windows that can be opened and closed add to the class' success because they can provide improved ventilation, and noise and temperature control.

Doors should be able to be latched tightly to prevent rattling from air currents. Then the facilitator can also use doors to control ventilation, temperature, and noise.

TEMPERATURE CONTROL

It is important to keep room temperature in a comfortable range for the majority of the clients. The ideal comfort range for groups in relaxation classes is between 66 and 70 degrees Farenheit. If the temperature is too warm, sweating and stuffiness can inhibit relaxation; too cool a room may hinder relaxation for some. We have found that, if one is to err on this matter, it is best to err toward a room that is too cool. Clients can use blankets or coats to keep warm in a cool room but little can be done to improve the conditions of a room that is too warm.

FURNISHINGS

When possible, furnishings should be aesthetically pleasing. Chairs should be comfortable, padded, and varied in size to accommodate the various-sized individuals in the class.

Tables, chairs, and desks should be movable, so the room can be altered for viewing films, small group activities, lectures, and practicing relaxation techniques. Bean bag chairs work well and provide good support, but they have several disadvantages. They are usually made of vinyl and can cause sweating in a warm room; they are usually large and take up large amounts of space; and they are hard to stack or store.

• • • • • • • • INSTRUCTIONAL POINTERS • • • • • • • •

1. *Check the room well in advance of conducting a class. This allows you to determine the appropriateness of the room for relaxation and gives you adequate time to make adjustments. You will also be able to determine the appropriate class size for the room.*

2. *Check the room for noise levels prior to conducting the class. Be sure to check the room on the same day of the week and at the same time that the class will meet. A room that is quiet at 9:00 a.m. on a Tuesday may not be quiet at 2:00 p.m. when your class is to be held.*

3. *Check the building master schedule to see what other groups are scheduled in adjacent and/or nearby rooms. Find out the size of these groups as well as the type of activities they plan to conduct in those rooms during your class time (lecture, dance, band practice, etc.).*

4. *Whenever conducting a relaxation class in a hotel/motel or convention setting, or if using relaxation techniques following a speech or banquet, discuss your*

needs with the hotel staff. Large group meetings in conference centers and in hotel/motel meeting rooms usually are located near a kitchen. Swinging doors, kitchen workers, cooking, dishwashers, etc., can be very distracting when people are relaxing. Advanced planning can help. Bring signs that say "Quiet Please" or "Relaxation Class in Progress" to remind the building staff of your special needs (see page 8 regarding signs). Place these signs in the hallways, kitchen, or other work areas when you are ready to practice relaxation techniques.

5. *Establish a secondary site whenever possible.*

6. *If acoustics are poor, a microphone may be necessary to amplify your voice so that all participants can hear.*

LIGHTING

Lighting should be moderate for relaxation practice. The harshness of bright lights interferes with relaxation. A completely dark room also should be avoided because you cannot see clients to monitor the success or difficulty they are having. Therefore, you will not be able to adjust your voice control to the clients' level of relaxation. In addition, people cannot see hazards if they are moving around, and the anxiety level of some clients will increase in the total absence of light.[1]

As a general rule, soft lighting is the best for a relaxation class. Lamps are generally more appropriate than overhead lighting. When conducting a stress management class, it is best to be able to control the lighting with a three-way lamp or a dimmer switch. Lighting can thus be controlled for the variety of activities which may be planned.

• • • • • • • •INSTRUCTIONAL POINTERS • • • • • • • •

1. If too bright lights cannot be dimmed or if over-head lights distract the clients when they are using a supine position, have clients lie under a chair or a table to diffuse the brightness of the lights.

2. When altering the lighting during a class (i.e., dimming or brightening, turning on or off), mention to the clients beforehand that "the lights will be turned on in approximately 10 seconds." This will remove anxiety and the stress of a changing environment for the clients.

NOISE

One of the most important criteria in room selection is quiet. The room should be as quiet as possible so that the clients can learn to relax under ideal circumstances. There are so many possible sources of noise interference that it is impossible to control all of them. The key to noise control is to control the controllable and to use the uncontrollable to your advantage.

CRITERIA FOR ROOM SELECTION IN REGARDS TO NOISE

To select a room that is as quiet as possible, choose one that is away from the major flow of traffic. People walking and talking in halls almost always distract individuals who are just beginning to learn relaxation techniques.

In addition, check the room and adjacent rooms or hallways for air conditioning units, heaters, fans, pop machines, water coolers and the like which may create noise interference. If possible, unplug the machines during class. If this is not possible, try to unplug them while clients are practicing techniques.

CHECK POINTS

Once again, advance planning can be helpful and can make a class easier to facilitate. Some common sources of noise interference that you can check for include:

1. *Telephones* - Telephones can interfere from adjacent rooms as well as the room in which you are teaching. If possible, have the phone(s) disconnected during the class. When this is not possible, try to reduce or muffle the sound by turning the bell sound down; covering the phone with a pillow or a blanket to reduce the sound; putting the phone in a desk drawer; opening the bottom of the phone and putting a cloth in the bell ringer mechanism; and, if the room is to be used on a regular basis, having an on/off switch installed for the ringer.

2. *Typewriters* - Check adjacent rooms for typewriters or computer printers which often make a good deal of noise. Typewriters and printers usually will not interfere with the class during lecture and small group activities, but they receive increased attention during relaxation. Make arrangements with these machine operators so they can be quiet during the five to ten minute periods that clients are practicing the relaxation techniques.

3. *Loudspeakers* - Be sure to check the room for loudspeakers or other similar systems over which announcements are made or music is played. This is particularly important when conducting classes in a hospital or a school setting. Make arrangements to have the loudspeaker turned off in the room in which you are conducting your class.

•••••••• INSTRUCTIONAL POINTERS •••••••

1.   Place signs in adjacent hallways reading "Quiet Please, Relaxation Class in Session." Be sure that the signs are placed perpendicular to the walls rather than parallel to or on the walls.   When the signs are perpendicular to the wall people can see them at a distance. This will alert people to be more quiet as they approach your room.

2.   If you cannot eliminate certain noises such as fans, air conditioners, and humming fluorescent lights use them to help the clients relax or teach the clients to disregard them (see page 14).

3.   If a loudspeaker cannot be turned off, check with the switchboard operator to find out when announcements are scheduled. Plan your breaks, lectures, films, or small group activities during these times. If announcements are made without a schedule, arrange for some type of warning such as a light tapping or blowing on the loudspeaker ten seconds before the announcement is made. This will give you ample time to prepare the clients for the upcoming announcement. It will also prevent them from being jarred out of a relaxed state by a loud, unexpected noise.

CHAPTER 2

VOICE CONTROL

In this chapter we examine factors regarding voice control to enhance your guiding techniques as a facilitator. When facilitating relaxation techniques, how something is said is just as important as what is said. The voice qualities displayed are of utmost importance in assisting clients in their relaxation efforts. Thus, this chapter is divided into two sections:

Messages, i.e., an overview of how messages are transmitted;

Voice Control, i.e., how the voice can and should be used to assist the clients to let go and relax.

MESSAGES

In most conversations, messages are transmitted in three different ways:

Word symbols are the actual words selected and used to express an idea, thought, or feeling.

Voice symbols are the tone, pitch and fluctuation of the voice.

Nonverbal symbols are usually referred to as body language or nonverbal communication.[1]

Any combination of these symbols accounts for how messages are conveyed from one individual to another. Research has revealed that word symbols account for only about 7% of a transmitted message. The voice symbols account for approximately 38% of the message, while nonverbal symbols account for 55%, or the major portion, of a transmitted message.

These nonverbal symbols are often referred to as body language. Nonverbal messages include dress, posture, eye contact, body tension, hand and body movements, mannerisms, facial expressions, confidence, overall appearance and the like. Often these messages are responsible for one's intuitive perception of an individual.

During relaxation techniques, a good portion of the nonverbal message is lost because the clients have their eyes closed. Some nonverbal communication such as appearance, dress and confidence of the facilitator displayed prior to clients closing the eyes still conveys a message. But, because the eyes are closed, much of the nonverbal message, such as posture, eye contact, body tension, hand and body movements, and facial expressions, is lost.

As a result, the verbal aspects of the message, the voice and the word symbols, become more important during relaxation than they do during normal conversations.

VOICE CONTROL

A good facilitator uses subtle features of volume and inflection changes to guide clients through a relaxation technique. For most people, these specific voice qualities do not occur naturally. Rather, facilitators must learn when and how to subtly vary the voice. With practice, these qualities develop naturally. In this section we examine voice qualities which, when used appropriately, can guide a client more quickly into a deeply relaxed state.

VOICE AND TONE QUALITIES
Beginning Tone

When you, the facilitator, begin to guide clients into a relaxed state, your voice tone and volume should approximate conversational tone and volume. This has a two-fold purpose.

1. It allows the clients to make the adjustments to the relaxation techniques gradually and in a non-threatening manner.
2. Since there will be some noise as clients adjust their positions, conversational tone and volume will allow clients to focus on

the facilitator's voice even in the presence of outside interference.

Reducing Tone and Volume as Relaxation is Elicited

As clients begin to relax, their hearing acuity increases. As a
facilitator, when you ascertain beginning signs of relaxation (see
pages 30 - 31 for specific relaxation signs), slowly reduce your voice
tone and volume according to the depth of perceived client relaxation. Be sure to position yourself properly in the room so that
when tone and volume are reduced all clients will be able to hear.
Reducing tone and volume does not imply a whisper. It means to
soften or to mellow the voice by reducing loudness. It is loudness
which may interfere with relaxation.

Tone and Volume Becoming Smooth, Quiet and Monotonous

As perceived relaxation deepens, your voice tone and volume
should take on a smooth, quiet, and, eventually, monotonous
quality. In fact, the tone and volume should become quite boring.
It is the monotony that assists the client to let go and to relax.
However, *do not remove all* intonation from your voice as this
sounds too artificial and can reduce your effectiveness as a
facilitator.

Increasing Tone and Volume When Needed

There are certain times, while guiding relaxation techniques,
when increased tone and volume are needed. Most often these
times are when you need to:

1. deal with distractions. Unwanted noises such as fans, clocks
   ticking, people walking by in adjacent halls, or a nearby conversation can disturb clients' relaxation efforts. When noise
   interference occurs, the volume and tone of your voice should
   be increased just enough to assure that clients will continue
   to focus on your voice and not be distracted by the extraneous noise.
2. increase tension. Your voice can be used to increase tension

in clients at appropriate times. Increased tone and volume are needed to bring clients out of the deeply relaxed state. A gradual increase in tone and volume during the last few sentences of a relaxation technique will alert clients that the technique is about to end. It will do this without abruptly concluding a peaceful and pleasant experience.[2]

As a facilitator you should keep in mind:

Reflect **relaxation** *in a* **reduced** *tone, volume and speed; reflect* **tension** *with* **increased** *tone, volume and speed.*

Timing Key Words with Exhalations

There are many sensations associated with each of the four phases of the breathing cycle. These various sensations are explained on page 59. For our purposes, it is enough to remember that the exhalation phase is the natural relaxation phase of the breathing cycle. As such, sensations associated with relaxation can be enhanced when the client times these sensations with the exhalation phase of the breathing cycle. Sensations to be timed with exhalations include, but are not limited to, the following: heaviness, warmth, sinking down, slowing down, patience, contentment, comfort, and letting go.

By timing these sensations or feelings with the relaxation phase of the breathing rhythm (the exhalation phase) a synergetic or compounding effect occurs. When this happens, the feelings are easier to feel, and the relaxed state enhances and deepens.

Extending Key Words

Another way to use your voice to assist clients in relaxation is to extend the key words. The key words include, but are not limited to, heaviness, warmth, sinking down, slowing down, patience, contentment, comfort, and letting go.

Sounding Natural, Confident and Competent

Each facilitator's vocal and tonal qualities are unique. There is no need to imitate another person's qualities. The facilitator should strive to be as natural sounding as possible.

•••••••••INSTRUCTIONAL POINTERS ••••••

1. *In a group setting, position yourself to speak toward the entire group. The voice will project better when volume and tone are reduced during relaxation.*

2. *In a large group setting, position yourself about one-third of the way into the group so that approximately two-thirds of the group are in front of you and the rest are behind you. Your voice will carry better to those in front of you, yet those behind you should be able to adequately hear when tone and volume are reduced. This is dependent, of course, on having an appropriately sized room. When guiding relaxation in a large room, a microphone with well-spaced speakers will provide the best voice control.*

3. *Since each room is acoustically different, check to see if clients can hear. We've found it helpful to have a hand signal that clients can use to signal the facilitator during a relaxation technique if they have difficulty in hearing. The hand signal works well because it alerts the facilitator to the problem but does not interfere with the relaxation of other clients.*

4. *Find out if clients have hearing difficulties. You may mention at the start of a class that clients with any hearing impairment should tell you about it during a break or at the conclusion of the first class. In a group setting, have the clients with hearing difficulties near you during the relaxation techniques. When tone and volume are reduced during the techniques, you may also want to project your voice toward those individuals.*

5. Be constantly aware of outside interference. Noises such as fans, air conditioners turning on, or people talking can interfere with relaxation efforts. As a facilitator, you have several options to eliminate or reduce this interference.

A. Make volume and tone adjustments as needed.

B. Continue talking by repeating and/or rephrasing the wording of a technique to maintain client attention.

C. Have fewer and shorter pauses if the technique is conducive to this type of adjustment.

D. Use the interference to help the clients relax. Have them focus on the noise and suggest the following:

"As the sounds get louder and louder feel yourself sinking down deeper and deeper into a more relaxed state."

E. Help focus the clients' attention within their bodies. You can say:

"Disregard all outside noises and keep your attention focused within your body because all that is important is what's happening within."

6. Tape a relaxation technique on a cassette and, prior to a class, play it at different volumes while you walk around the room. Try to determine how sounds travel within the room while you alter volume and tone.

7. Do not take on overly dramatic or theatrical vocal qualities. Clients will then focus on the intonation changes rather than on the technique itself.[3]

8. Do not talk so loud that you interfere with relaxation or so soft that the clients must work at *hearing your. Both will hinder relaxation efforts of the clients.*

9. *When reading techniques extend the key words that are written with a hyphen between each letter. For example, when reading "feel the body s-l-o-w-i-n-g d-o-w-n" you as a facilitator would extend the words "slowing down" to assist the clients to relax.*

PACE QUALITIES

Beginning Pace

As with tone and volume, the beginning pace should be similar to the pace of a relaxed conversation. The pace should be fast enough to keep clients' thoughts from wandering, yet it should be slow enough to let clients feel, sense, or experience sensations of relaxation.

Reducing Pace as Relaxation is Elicited

The pace of the technique is reduced as the clients begin to relax. Pace reduction should occur over a period of time so that it is gradual and unnoticeable to the clients. Ideally, pacing should be based on the clients' level of relaxation. When working in a one-to-one relationship, the clients' breathing rate can be used to establish the pacing of the technique. Time key words to the exhalation phase of the breathing cycle and adjust the wording and pacing accordingly (see Chapter 3 on wording). In a large group setting, pace should be based on the average state of relaxation of the clients.

Pausing

Pauses are an important part of pacing. If appropriately inserted in the phrasing of a technique, pauses will help the clients relax. Generally, pauses occur at the end of phrases or sentences where sensations associated with relaxation are mentioned. A key factor in voice control is to prepare the clients for the pauses without interfering with the relaxed state. To do this, decrease the intonation of the words preceding the pause. This decrease of intonation implies an upcoming pause and the client will expect or anticipate it.

Remember, pauses which occur in the middle of a phrase or a sentence or without the proper intonation changes are often distracting. They can actually bring some clients out of a relaxed state.

• • • • • • • • INSTRUCTIONAL POINTERS • • • • • • •

1. *When working one-to-one, use the client's breathing rate to set the pace and determine the length of the pauses. To do this, observe the inhalation and the exhalation of air at the diaphragm or by watching the rising and falling of the chest.*

2. *Do not guide too fast or have the pauses too short. When first guiding relaxation techniques, most facilitators tend to believe they are going too slow and pausing too long when, in fact, the opposite is usually true.*

3. *The best way to check your pacing is to tape several relaxation techniques at what you consider to be the proper pace. Then, relax to the tapes yourself. You can judge whether or not the pacing is appropriate, too fast or too slow.*

CHAPTER 3

PROPER WORDING FOR RELAXATION TECHNIQUES

The actual words the facilitator uses when guiding relaxation techniques can either assist the client in relaxing or inhibit the client's ability to relax. It is important to convey certain feelings, sensations, and subconscious messages to clients. The proper selection and use of words to convey these messages make the facilitator's job easier, more successful and more rewarding. As such, it is important to consider the actual words used and the possible effect they may have on the clients when developing, writing and paraphrasing relaxation techniques.

This chapter is divided into two sections:

1. proper wording for techniques, and
2. words that should be eliminated.

WORDING THAT ALLOWS CLIENTS TO MAINTAIN CONTROL

If a relaxation program is to be successful, the clients must realize that they are in control of themselves at all times. If they sense that *they are doing* the relaxation rather than *it being done to them*, they will be more likely to perform a technique during class and subsequently be more successful when performing techniques on their own.

In a relaxed state, words can have a greater impact on the subconscious mind. Because of this it is important to use words and phrasing that permit the clients to maintain control during relaxation. The examples in the first column illustrate commonly used phrases or words that imply the facilitator is in charge, in control or in a position of authority. In the second column the same ideas are expressed in a way that allows the client to remain in control.

Avoid phrases like:	Change to phrases like:
"Close your eyes . . ."	"Permit yourself to close your eyes . . ." "When ready, allow your eyes to close."
"I want you to . . ."	"Allow yourself to . . ." "At this time, permit/allow" "When ready . . ."

WORDING THAT SHOULD BE AVOIDED

ELIMINATE WORDS AND PHRASES THAT DEMAND WORK

Certain phrases and words suggest work or effort. This is contrary to what you want to do during a relaxation technique because a passive attitude is an important prerequisite to relaxation. As a facilitator, attempt to change phrases and words so that the feeling of effort is removed whenever possible.

Avoid phrases and words like:	Change to phrases and words like:
"Try to feel . . ."	"Feel, sense and experience..." "Allow yourself to feel . . ."
"Concentrate on . . . "	"Permit yourself to focus your attention on . . . " "At this time, allow . . ."

ELIMINATE WORDS AND PHRASES
WITH A NEGATIVE CONNOTATION

Many phrases used in relaxation have more than one meaning and, if taken out of context, can evoke a negative reaction for some people. When this occurs clients often feel angry, frustrated, uneasy, stressed, or they suddenly develop a lack of interest in the class. Ironically, clients often do not know why their feelings have changed. They may be unaware that the change is a result of a subconscious, rather than a conscious, response to the words or phrases used. To prevent this from occurring, use common sense and place yourself in the position of clients by examining the words and phrases used.

Avoid Phrases that Refer to a Physical Weakness or Handicap

Avoid using terms or phrases like "feel the muscles drooping down..." or "feel the muscles sagging...." These phrases invariably evoke a negative response, especially in older and overweight people. These examples can be rephrased more positively to "feel the muscles smoothing out..." or "feel the gentle pull of gravity exert itself on...." This is especially important when referring to the muscles of the neck, abdomen, face or upper arms.

Even terms like heavy or heaviness can evoke an unpleasant response in some people. Heavy can be a feeling that is uncomfortable or is associated with being overweight or obese. This is *important to remember when dealing with obese or overweight clients or when teaching relaxation to a group involved in a weight control program.* Since the feeling of heaviness, which indicates relaxation, is important, it is hard to disregard the feeling during a relaxation technique. When possible and appropriate, consider using the terms "comfortably heavy" or "feel the gentle pull of gravity exert itself on the ...." This takes some of the bite out of the phrase while allowing clients to perceive the same sensation. [1]

AVOID WORDS AND PHRASES
THAT CONNOTE TENSION

Other often-used phrases refer to excessive stress, tension or strain. Phrases such as "tense the muscles to the breaking point" or "strain the muscles" are not helpful and should be avoided whenever possible, even during progressive relaxation. Simply say "tense the muscles" or "increase the tension...." There is no need to overemphasize the tension; a facilitator can elicit the appropriate response with these phrases.

PHRASES TO USE

Now that we've examined phrases that should not be used, let's consider some phrases that enhance relaxation. The following terms and phrases help clients perceive that they, not the facilitator, are evoking the relaxation response. This perception creates a sense of control by the clients and further establishes a trusting relationship with the facilitator, which in itself is useful when teaching relaxation.

"Allow yourself..."
"Permit yourself..."
"When ready..."
"At this time..."
"Let go"
"Feel"
"Experience"
"Feel, sense, and experience..."
"Calm"
"Tranquility"
"Serenity"
"Peace"
"Contentment"

"Relaxed"

"Comfortable (or) comforting"

"Patience"

"Notice"

"Discover"

"Find"

Although this list is not all inclusive, it serves as a starting point in selecting words and phrases that are appropriate to use when leading relaxation techniques.

• • • • • • • • • INSTRUCTIONAL POINTERS • • • • • • •

1.   *Examine each technique in terms of how the wording may affect an obese, overweight, handicapped, or older client; then alter the wording accordingly.*

2.   *Keep a file of appropriate words or phrases and read through it on a regular basis to reemphasize those terms.*

3.   *Regularly examine your wording by taping and listening to techniques. It's easy to slip back into old ways.*

CHAPTER 4

RECOGNIZING TENSION AND RELAXATION IN CLIENTS

It is important for the facilitator of stress management classes to be able to recognize the signs and the symptoms of stress and of relaxation. The sections in this chapter examine both.

SIGNS AND SYMPTOMS OF STRESS

It is important to recognize that stress in one's life can be caused by a variety of factors including psychological stressors, sociological stressors, biological stressors (e.g., viruses), environmental stressors (e.g., temperature changes). These stressors are perceived by the mind (our perceptions are important in determining stressors) and translated by the brain which instructs the rest of the body how to respond to the stressor.[1]

The research on stress reactions indicates there are certain signs and symptoms common to stress and that these signs and symptoms can eventually lead to diseases if left unmanaged. Many of these symptoms, such as changes in blood levels of adrenaline, corticoids, ACTH, blood eosinophils, and blood lipids, are found through laboratory evaluations. These symptoms are important because they alert the individual that the body is under stress and because they can also be used to measure the physiological impact of a stressor on an individual.[2]

However, laboratory evaluations are not often used when conducting stress management programs. Therefore, other signs (something that can be seen by someone else, such as a facilitator) may be more important for assessing progress than would symptoms (something the individual alone can feel or which can be detected through laboratory tests). Actually the body does display outward signs of stress that can be perceived by the individual and/or others without laboratory evaluation. These signs, which can be noticed by the individual or by an observant facilitator, can be effective in recognizing distress in the body.

Individuals with satisfactory sensory awareness will be able to notice the body responding to a stressor. However, many individuals may not recognize that their own body is under stress until a stress related problem occurs, physically or psychologically. When this happens, close friends and associates may recognize the tension, indicated by changes in mood, attitude or behavior, before the individual does.

Many signs can be noticed by an observant facilitator in a counseling or classroom setting. The key, then, is for a facilitator to recognize the signs of stress and share them with the client. With this knowledge the client will be able to recognize stress more readily and thus be able to take appropriate actions more quickly. This information can also be used to measure the success of the intervention strategies. If unsuccessful, the facilitator can alter the approach.

SIGNS MOST LIKELY TO BE SEEN BY A FACILITATOR IN A SESSION WITH A CLIENT

The following list includes recognizable signs of tension likely to be seen by a facilitator in a stress management class or counseling session. Although these signs can be perceived by the client, they frequently are not. These signs may indicate that the individual is coming to the session under stress or, if they appear during a relaxation technique, that the person may be having difficulties with that strategy. Keep in mind, however, that no one or two signs alone definitely mean a person is under stress. But, in a broad sense, the more numerous the signs observed, the more accurate your assessment that the individual is responding with significant stress symptoms.

Physical
Increased breathing rate
Perspiration
underarm
face
hands
Muscle tension
shoulders held high
clenching of the jaw
clenching the fist
frowning; grimacing
Breathing
hyperventilation
chest breathing
fast breathing rate
Poor circulation (cold hands)
Skin conditions
rashes
hives
itchy skin
Eyes
rapid eye movement
staring
Speaking
excessive talking
excessive variations in voice level
rapid speaking
Nervous actions
biting lips
biting nails
rocking motion
fast body movements
hand/finger movements
tapping fingers or cracking knuckles

twisting hair with fingers
bouncing knees
toe tapping
chewing on objects (e.g., pens, pencils)
compulsive gum chewing
General fatigue

Emotional
Inappropriate laughter
Lack of empathy
short tempered
easily angered
grouchiness
constant complaining
Helplessness
crying
pouting
Hostility
Depression
Unable to relax or "let go" [3]

SYMPTOMS OF STRESS FELT BY THE CLIENT BUT UNLIKELY TO BE SEEN BY OTHERS FIRST

An individual is likely to perceive many symptoms of stress that are not recognized or seen by others unless indicated to them by the individual. Some symptoms indicate minor manifestations of stress; others indicate that the body has been reacting to stressors for long periods of time and is now suffering from one of the stress related diseases (e.g., ulcers).

Physical
Muscle tension
neck
shoulders
bruxism (grinding of the teeth)

tightness in the stomach
low back ache
leg tension and pain
Headaches
  migraine
  tension
Digestive problems
  nausea and vomiting
  frequent bowel movements
  diarrhea
  constipation
  ulcers
  heartburn
  spastic bowel
  ulcerative colitis
Breathing problems
  hyperventilation
  dry mouth
Cardiovascular problems
  increased heart rate
  pounding in the chest
  chest pain
Lack of energy
  desire to sleep constantly
Eye problems
  double vision
  blurred vision
Ringing in the ears
Speaking problems
  dry mouth (cotton mouth)
  "lumps" in the throat
  stuttering
Nervousness
  can't sit still

nervous actions
nervous tremor in the hands
Increased energy
decreased perception of fatigue
Increased drug usage
alcohol
compulsive smoking
overconsumption of caffeine
others (both legal and illegal)
Eating habits
compulsive eating
lack of appetite
Sleep problems
restless sleep
insomnia
Premenstrual tension and missed menstrual cycle

Emotional
Mental disorganization
lack of concentration
feeling of inferiority
frustration
Nightmare dreams
Allergy symptoms
Lack of empathy
short tempered
grouchy
constant complaining
mistrust
Helplessness
lack of motivation
withdrawal
fear of the unknown
hopelessness (people against you)
increased dependency

urge to hide
insecurity
feeling abandoned
anxiety
Feeling of wanting to be physical
   slamming doors
   throwing things
   striking or kicking objects
Depression
Unable to relax
Panicky feeling

Intellectual (Cognitive)
   Mental blocks
      forget common names
      memory lapses
      indecision
      inability to organize thoughts
      mind goes blank
      inability to concentrate
   Increased fantasies
   Procrastination
   Loss of interest
   Escapism[4]

SIGNS OF STRESS SEEN BY OTHERS IN DAILY LIVING SITUATIONS

The following group of signs of stress are likely to be seen by others such as family, friends, roommates, and peers. These are the symptoms that are displayed in the individual's overt behavior and are usually seen in the home and work setting. They are also likely to appear spontaneously throughout the day.

Depressed mood
Excessive drinking
General irritability
High absenteeism
Apathy
Frequent accidents
Frequent illnesses
Unusual aggressive or passive behavior
Neurotic behavior
Reduced decision-making skills
Job dissatisfaction
Increased interpersonal conflict
Decreased job performance
Decreased sexual activity

STRESS RELATED DISEASES

Left unchecked, stress can progressively affect the body until physiological changes occur which can lead to stress related health problems. Although some of these changes were already listed as symptoms of stress, their occurrence can lead to an acute or chronic problem that can threaten one's enjoyment of life as well as threaten life itself. The following list includes stress related diseases and problems that have been linked directly or indirectly with stress.

Hypertension
Depression
Coronary heart disease
Peptic ulcer
Asthma
Diabetes
Mental health problems
Substance abuse
Accidents
Low back pain

Terminal renal failure
Skin rashes
Tuberculosis
Multiple sclerosis
Cancer
Childhood streptococcal infections
Suicides
Child abuse
Headaches
Obesity
Alcoholism
Drug dependency
Spastic colon

SIGNS AND SYMPTOMS OF RELAXATION

While signs and symptoms of tension are important, it is equally, if not more, important for the facilitator to recognize signs and symptoms that indicate clients are relaxing. During relaxation, changes take place in the neural pathways which produce both signs (observable) and symptoms (non-observable) that relaxation is occurring.

VISIBLE SIGNS OF RELAXATION

While guiding a client the facilitator should be watching for signs of relaxation. Table 4-1 lists the signs which can be seen by an observant facilitator and this knowledge can be used to enhance the clients' success in the class.

While guiding a client the facilitator should be watching for visible signs of relaxation. This monitoring enables the facilitator to (1) use the client's breathing rhythm to establish the relaxation technique pace while guiding (pacing); (2) change the relaxation technique phrases to address tension areas observed in the client (e.g., tight jaw, elevated shoulder, furrowed brow); (3) notice when a client has difficulty with a particular technique or is unable to perform the exercise because of excessive stress levels; (4) use the signs so as to adapt the voice control (tone, pauses, pacing, volume, etc.) to the client's level of relaxation; and (5) assess the level of relaxation in the client.

Using the knowledge the facilitator obtains from these visible signs is often the difference between a good facilitator and an excellent one. The signs provided by the client help the facilitator become a better guide.

Table 4 - 1

Visible Signs of Relaxation

Face and Neck
    Forehead muscles smooth, not furrowed
    Eyelids smooth
    Facial muscles less well defined (wrinkle lines less well defined)
    Jaw slightly opened, not clenched (masseter and temporalis muscles not
        prominent or bulging)
    Neck muscles less well defined
    Swallowing more frequent
    Carotid pulse is less visible and slower
Breathing
    Shift from chest breathing to abdominal breathing
    Lengthened time between exhalation and inspiration
    Exhalation under less muscle control; a more passive, quicker process as the
        lungs' natural elasticity allows the air to escape
    Sounds of inhalation and exhalation become more pronounced
Hands
    Palms of hands are a consistent pink, not speckled or white
    Fingernail beds are a consistent pink without bands of white
Posture
    Areas of the body succumb to the pull of gravity
    Shoulders drop
    Legs separate slightly (if seated)
    Knees slightly bent, not locked (if lying supine)
    Toes point outwards more (if lying supine)

NON-OBSERVABLE SYMPTOMS OF RELAXATION

During relaxation there are many things occurring within the mind and body of the client that are not directly visible to the facilitator (see Table 4-2). The facilitator can get further information by having clients voluntarily share some of their own observations of the relaxation process and the state of relaxation they reached (see pages 222 - 223 for further information on processing techniques). Since the facilitator knows these are symptoms associated with relaxation, the symptoms can serve as reinforcement of clients' efforts to relax. The facilitator can also select several symptoms and ask the clients if they noticed them during the period of relaxation. Many times clients experience a symptom of relaxation but forget it until mentioned by the facilitator. Sharing in this manner further assists the facilitator in determining what exercises are beneficial to clients as well as in noting difficulties that arise.

Table 4 - 2

Non-Observable Symptoms of Relaxation

Body Sensations:

    Increasing warmth, heaviness, tingling

    Sinking down, floating, drifting

    Lightness, weightlessness, airiness

    Alteration of kinesthetic sense (extremities cannot be sensed, extremities do
       not feel attached to the body)

Disassociation:

    Noise interference is no longer distracting

    Loss of perception of heart rate, breathing or other body sensations

    Loss of perception of supporting environment and its characteristics

    "Blank spots" - not knowing where the mind was the last few seconds

Time perception alters (time expands or contracts)

Physiological Alterations:

    Increased salivation

    Heart rate decreased, strength of heartbeats less pronounced

    Growling in the stomach, increased awareness of hunger or thirst

    Awareness of gas moving through the intestine

    Increased awareness of need to void the urinary bladder

    Breathing is more relaxed and natural

    Muscles feel less tense, more relaxed

CHAPTER 5

COMMONLY ASKED QUESTIONS

JUST EXACTLY WHAT IS RELAXATION?

Relaxation is a systematic means of bringing about physiological changes in the body that are opposite from the stress response. Relaxation exercises serve as a systematic means to relax both the mind and the body. You are able to cruise in neutral - a state where the body and mind are restored from the wear and tear of living.

WHY SHOULD A PERSON TAKE TIME TO RELAX?

Studies have shown that people who relax regularly are less anxious, psychologically and physiologically more stable, and have greater control over their lives. People have also reported sleeping better, feeling less fatigued at the end of the day, being more productive at work, and getting along better with others. Studies have also demonstrated beneficial results in controlling many of the stress-related diseases.

HOW MUCH TIME DOES ONE HAVE TO SPEND RELAXING TO ACHIEVE BENEFITS?

In our hectic, fast-paced society, any time spent allowing the mind and body to recoup is beneficial. For maximum benefits, we recommend two ten-minute sessions or one twenty-minute session every day. If you notice increased tension during the day, periodic three- to five-minute sessions can also be extremely helpful.

WHEN IS THE BEST TIME TO RELAX?

The best time to relax is when you perceive a need to slow down or to get out from under the pressure cooker. Some individuals prefer to relax in the early morning; others mid-morning; still others late in the afternoon. Each person will need to decide when and how relaxation best can be incorporated into a daily schedule without causing stress. If there is one general rule of when not to relax, it is immediately after eating. Otherwise, it's your choice.

DO I NEED SOMEONE OR SOMETHING TO GUIDE ME?

Although a trained relaxation technician or a relaxation tape can be beneficial when learning to relax, they are not necessary. Actually, each person allows relaxation to occur; it does not happen because of the technician or tape. Learn to listen to and guide yourself through relaxation exercises. In this way, you can relax whenever and wherever you are - not only if there is a tape recorder available.

ARE RELAXATION AND SLEEP THE SAME?

No! Both sleep and relaxation are altered states of consciousness but at different levels. Sleep can be physically restless and a time for the mind to work out the stresses of life. During deep relaxation, there is little or no anxiety. Actually, deep relaxation is even more restful than sleep. However, relaxation is not a substitute for sleep, nor is sleep a substitute for relaxation. The body and mind require both.

CAN RELAXATION BE HARMFUL?

In a general sense, no! It is no more harmful than praying for the same period of time. Anyone taking medication, especially prescribed by a physician, should check with a physician before embarking on a relaxation program. Occasionally, the mixture of chemicals and deep relaxation may be counterproductive to health. The best advice here is to use your best judgment and, if there is any question whatever, call your health-care provider.

WHAT CAN I DO ABOUT DISTRACTING THOUGHTS WHILE I'M TRYING TO RELAX?

The first thing to recognize is that there will be times when your mind will wander while you are trying to relax, especially when you are under a great deal of stress and/or time deadlines. Should you try to force these thoughts away or become irritated by them, tension will be created and the ability to relax lessened. When these thoughts occur, remain passive, acknowledge them, and let them serve as a cue for you to return first to exhalations and then continue the relaxation exercise. With practice you will soon discover that the distracting thoughts will become fewer and you will be able to relax without the mind wandering.

WILL RELAXING EVERY DAY LEAD TO LAZINESS?

The core of the question seems to be, "Will taking time to relax make me less productive?" No! Several studies indicate that people who take five or ten minutes to relax during coffee breaks or other planned times during the day are actually more productive than those who don't. Taking time to allow the body to slow down, reduce fatigue, and energize allows for better pacing, increased stamina, and increased work efficiency.[1]

IS IT ADVISABLE TO PRACTICE RELAXATION
TECHNIQUES AFTER EATING A MEAL?

It is permissable to practice relaxation techniques after a light meal. However, the body does undergo greater physiological changes while digesting a larger or heavier meal. The stomach lining produces a greater amount of acid to digest a larger meal, and, in the process of producing the hydrochloric acid to aid digestion, it releases an alkaline product into the blood. This alkaline product can alter the pH of the blood, making it slightly more alkaline than normal. This is called the alkaline tide. The increased alkalinity of the blood does have a mild effect on the brain, leading to a more drowsy, sleepy state. Therefore, practicing relaxation techniques after a heavy meal may enhance this sleepy state and lead to a brief nap rather than to a deeply relaxed state.

CHAPTER 6

BASIC RELAXATION POSITIONS

SELECTING A POSITION

When preparing to relax, it is important to select a body position that will not hinder relaxation. The position selected should not cause muscular tension, inhibit circulation, invite cramps or provoke unnecessary movement or effects. The position should enhance a person's ability to "let go" and relax. The following suggestions should help clients select a position for their relaxation program.

1. The position selected *must meet the clients needs*. Everyone is different, and no one position or combination of positions will serve everyone. Have clients select and/or adapt a position to meet their needs, preferences and physical requirements.

2. The position should be comfortable and have a minimum of muscular tension. To decrease the muscular tension required to maintain the body in place, the position should provide maximum support for as many body parts as possible.

3. The body should be well aligned, that is, the right side of the body should be in the same position as the left side. This allows for greater stability when in a deeply relaxed state.

4. The arms and legs should be supported. This will help ensure a minimum amount of muscular tension.

5. The arms and hands, and the legs and feet, should not be crossed or touching. When body parts cross or touch, sweating, impaired circulation, limbs falling asleep, and cramping often occur. All of these interfere with relaxation.

6. It is easiest to learn the skills in positions that provide maximum support for the body, i.e., back-lying, easy chair, side position and recliner positions.

7. After mastering relaxation, practice in positions that provide minimum support. With practice, you can relax just as deeply in minimum support positions, thus increasing the number of settings in which you can relax (e.g., airplanes, bus terminals, sitting on a bench or chair, riding in a car).[1]

MAXIMUM SUPPORT POSITIONS

Figure 6 - 1

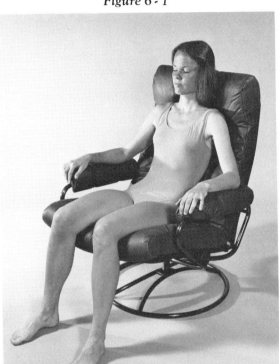

EASY CHAIR POSITION

This position requires a high-back chair. To assume the position, the client should sit in the chair, lean back, and allow the chair to support his or her head, back, buttocks, and thighs. The arms should rest on the arms of the chair or on the lap, and the feet and legs should be spread comfortably with the feet flat on the floor. Have the clients adjust the position so that they are comfortable. This is a position of maximum support and can be used effectively when first learning to relax.

Figure 6 - 2

BACK LYING POSITION

To assume the back lying position, clients should lay in a supine position with their arms resting comfortably at the sides with the elbows in a slightly flexed position. The legs should be comfortably spread apart. Many people prefer to use a pillow under the head, but only a very small one should be used so tension is not created in the head and neck region.

• • • • • • • •INSTRUCTIONAL POINTER • • • • • • • •

Rather than pillows a small towel rolled up or folded over and placed under the neck places the head in an excellent position (note the towel in Figure 6-2).

Variations of the Back Lying Position

Arm and shoulder support

Pillows or blankets are used under the arms and/or shoulders to eliminate tension in the chest and shoulder region. Arm and shoulder support is especially helpful when lying on a hard surface such as a floor.

Figure 6 - 3

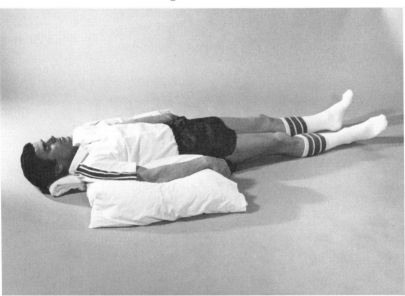

•••••••• INSTRUCTIONAL POINTER ••••••

Women that have recently had a mastectomy have reported that this variation of the back lying position is one of the most comfortable until the soreness from the surgery subsides.

Figure 6 - 4

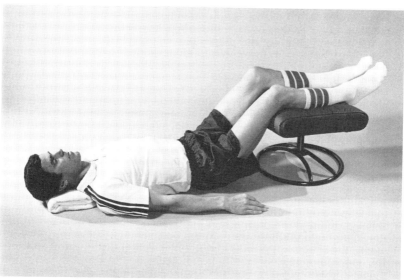

Knee support

Individuals with back problems may have to elevate the knees to reduce low back pain or tightness. The elevation of the knees flattens the lower back and reduces the tension. A chair can be used as shown in Figure 6-4 or pillows or blankets can be used as shown in Figure 6-5. In either case, support must exist under the knees so that the knees are bent. The elevation must be of an appropriate height so that the clients are comfortable.

Figure 6 - 5

• • • • • • • • INSTRUCTIONAL POINTERS • • • • • • • •

1. *Emphasize that the support must be under the knees and that the knees must be bent to flatten the back.*

2. *When clients are using a chair to elevate the knees the chair must be drawn tight against the back of the thigh to provide support directly under the knees.*

SIDE POSITION

The side position is a very individualized position which takes adjustments to get used to. This position is often the choice of pregnant women during the later months of pregnancy. Other individuals that cannot get comfortable when lying on their backs also use this variation.

•••••••••• INSTRUCTIONAL POINTER ••••••••

Have clients try the side position with as many variations as possible (i.e., pillow under the head, a pillow between the knees, one leg forward, the other leg forward, etc.). Each person is unique and and this is one position which requires finding a variation which fits the clients needs for comfort.

Figure 6 - 6

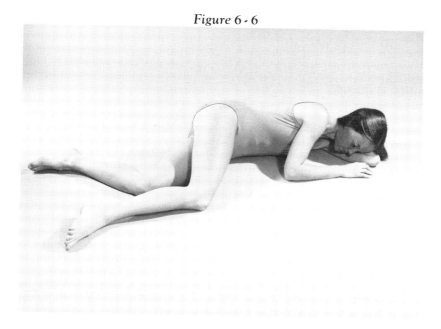

RECLINER POSITION

This is similar to the easy chair position. The use of a reclining chair offers many adjustable positions, all of which offer excellent support and are helpful when learning to relax.

Figure 6 - 7

• • • • • • • • • •INSTRUCTIONAL POINTER • • • • • • • •

Recliners come in a variety of sizes and a size that is comfortable for one person may not be comfortable for another.

MINIMUM SUPPORT POSITIONS

FORWARD LEANING SITTING POSITION

This position requires active use of various muscles to maintain it. Thus, tension exists because the body is not entirely supported by the chair. However, the position can be used in a variety of places since it does not require back support.

To assume this position, the client should sit down on a chair, bench, toilet seat or some other place where support for the buttocks is provided. The arms and hands should be supported by the legs, and the feet should be comfortably spread apart and flat on the ground. The head can either hang forward or, if that is not comfortable, the client can lean back until the head is balanced upright with as little tension as possible.

Figure 6 - 8

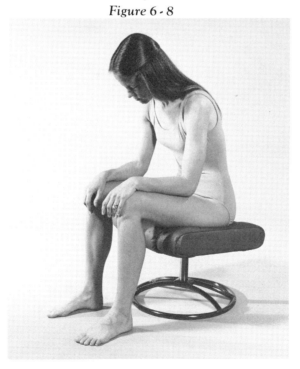

UPRIGHT SITTING POSITION

To assume the upright sitting position, some type of back support is needed in addition to support for the buttocks. Support is provided for the lower back and the buttocks by the chair and for the feet by the floor. The arms and the hands should rest on the upper legs or on the arms of the chair. The feet should be flat on the floor and comfortably spread apart. The head can hang forward or be held upright, whichever is more comfortable.[2]

Figure 6 - 9

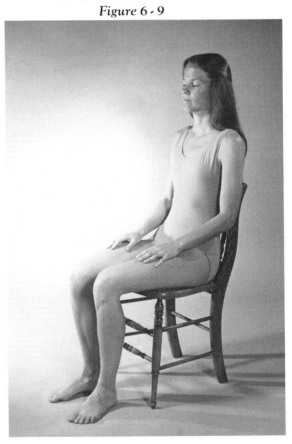

CHAPTER 7

SENSORY AWARENESS TRAINING: A PRELUDE TO RELAXATION

Tune in! Feel! Listen to your body as it communicates to you. What is it saying? What is it trying to say? Why am I not hearing? Sensory awareness training focuses on these questions. Sensory awareness training is based on the assumption that human beings, in pursuit of becoming civilized, have learned to disregard bodily messages. With the multitude of external stimuli affecting us daily, many individuals have simply lost the ability to perceive and interpret their own vital signs. Yet, the array of stimuli bombarding the individual elicits corresponding bodily reactions which may not even reach the conscious level. Learning to read vital signs, messages which are transferred into bodily reactions, means giving more attention to a narrowed field of consciousness and the feelings and sensations of the present.

In sensory awareness training there is no search for the cause of these perceived sensations. Likewise, there is no criticism or value judgment formed about the sensations once they are noticed. It is only important to feel, sense, or experience the sensations. The training is merely one of tuning in, listening, and acknowledging what exists within the body.

DEFINITIONS OF SENSORY AWARENESS

There are many definitions of sensory awareness with implications toward training individuals to become more aware of their senses. We present two of them to enhance your understanding of sensory awareness as it may apply to your vocation, clientele, or teaching.

Keen observation, differentiation of perceptions, and a wide range of sensitivity . . . temperatures, textures, weight of objects and parts of the body, and the sensations of contact with objects.[1]

An increased consciousness of sensory perceptions and sensations,[2] *for example, muscular tension, pressure, gravity, temperature changes, twitching, and vague feelings of happiness, peace, contentment, patience, comfort, and security.*

SAMPLE SENSORY AWARENESS TECHNIQUES

Almost all relaxation techniques include some type of sensory awareness. Table 7-1 presents a representative list of perceptions and sensations that clients most frequently report with the specific technique noted. Although the table attempts to classify the most frequent perceptions and sensations reported by clients, the fact remains that clients feel or perceive what *they* feel or perceive. As such, the relaxation facilitator should approach sensory awareness training with a sense of creativity and be prepared to receive feedback of a number of perceived sensations as clients share their individual experiences.

The majority of relaxation techniques and sensory awareness techniques listed in Table 7-1 can be found in *How To Relax: A Holistic Approach to Stress Management* or in other relaxation training manuals. Two additional techniques, Partner Sensory Awareness and Finger Tip Sensory Awareness, are presented here. As you read through the descriptions of these techniques and practice them yourself, note how they provide for exploration of sensations. Further, be aware of how the technique is presented to assist the client in narrowing the field of consciousness.

Table 7 - 1

Perceived Sensations \ Relaxation Techniques	Partner Sensory Awareness	Fingertips	*Hand-Clench	*Stand	*Breathing-Inhalation	*Breathing-Exhalation	*Body-search	*Supporting Environment	*Bezola's Autoanalysis	*Progressive Relaxation	*Benson's Relaxation Response	*Visualization	Practical Techniques	Sequential Relaxation	Schultz Standard Autogenic Training
Hardness	X		X	X	X			X	X						
Dryness					X				X						
Expansion (chest region)					X				X						
Tightening	X		X	X	X			X	X			X			
Ascending-upward/body levitating/movement	X				X		X			X					
Alertness					X					X					
Preparation for action					X					X					
Lightness	X				X			X	X	X	X				X
Sinking down/Descending					X			X	X	X	X	X	X	X	X
Letting go/Release of tension	X		X		X			X		X	X	X	X	X	X
Twitching			X				X		X	X			X		
Heartbeat/Pulse/Thumping		X			X		X								X
Slowing down					X			X	X	X	X			X	X
Lengthening of breath					X					X				X	X
Blending of body parts		X	X				X			X	X	X		X	X
Heaviness	X				X		X		X	X			X	X	X
Warmth	X				X		X		X	X		X		X	X
Moisture					X										X
Calmness					X				X	X	X			X	X
Weakness				X					X	X					X
Patience/Slowing down					X	X		X	X	X			X	X	X
Peace					X				X	X	X		X		
Concentration	X	X		X	X		X	X		X	X			X	X
Boredom/Monotony					X				X	X			X		
Satisfaction					X							X	X		
Contentment/Comfort	X				X	X	X	X	X	X	X	X	X	X	X
Contemplation										X					X
Alertness/Invigoration/Refreshment				X						X					
Increased tension/Tightness	X		X		X		X	X	X			X			
Coolness				X			X					X			X

*Complete exercise descriptions, and in most cases perceived sensations, are presented separately in J. Curtis and R. Detert, *How To Relax: A Holistic Approach to Stress Management* (Palo Alto, CA: Mayfield Publishing Company, 1981).

PARTNER SENSORY AWARENESS

Sit upright in a straight armchair. Be aware of where you are touching the chair.

Take all possible support from the back of the chair, its arms, and its seat.

Keep the feet comfortably and securely on the floor and, during exhalations, let the tensions flow down and out of the body into the chair.

Feel the support from the chair and relax with each exhalation.

Will you permit me to put my hand lightly on your shoulder? Can you feel your shoulder underneath my hand?

I am now going to gently take away my hand. Can you feel your shoulder?

I will repeat this while you focus your attention on your shoulder. Sense your shoulder; feel your shoulder; experience your shoulder. I am putting my hand there again. Can you feel my hand? Can you feel your shoulder under my hand?

Again, keep your mind on that shoulder while I take away my hand. Keep your mind on that shoulder while you feel it, sense it, experience it. Compare it with your other shoulder. Can you feel any difference? Can you describe that difference?

Now I will put my hand heavily on your shoulder. How does my hand feel now? How does my hand feel when it is lifted to the position where it touches your shoulder only lightly? How does it feel, if held just above your shoulder, where it loses touch but is close enough that you can feel its warmth?

Now flex and stretch and invigorate yourself.[3]

•••••••••INSTRUCTIONAL POINTERS•••••••

1. *Have clients remove jackets, sweaters, or other bulky clothing prior to the beginning of this technique. Too much clothing can interfere with assisting in the creating of sensations.*

2. *Consider using hand signals during the partner sensory awareness training to assure that all clients are doing the same movement at the same time.*

3. *Prior to starting this technique with a group of clients, explain that the person who is seated is to respond, verbally and in a concise manner, to all questions to the person behind him/her. The seated person is to respond to that person as if he/she were responding to you the facilitator.*

4. *Observe correct hand placement and movement on the shoulder of the seated person.*

5. *During the second time through the technique (allowing the other partner to experience the technique), encourage the person who is standing to perceive any sensations while the hand is placed on the shoulder.*

FINGER TIP SENSORY AWARENESS

Sit upright in a chair with elbows resting comfortably on a table or your knees.

Place all of your fingertips together with a little pressure so that the entire fleshy parts are in contact with each other.

Take a slightly deeper breath in and as you exhale allow your eyes to close.

Listen to yourself breathe for several exhalations and r-e-l-a-x as you exhale.

Focus your attention now on your index fingers at the exact spot where they come together. Feel, sense, and experience this spot. Allow yourself to feel the small but noticeable pulse in the fingertips.

And now focus your attention on your middle fingers at the exact spot where they come together. Repeat the feel, sense, and experience for each of the three remaining fingers. Allow several exhalations per pair of fingers.

Next allow your mind to perceive or experience some perception or sensation as you spontaneously focus on something interesting about your fingers (e.g., they have become one rather than two distinct fingers, pulse is stronger in one set of fingers, pulse disappeared, tingling, warmth, etc.).

After several more exhalations, and when you are ready, flex-stretch-inhale and open your eyes.

•••••••• INSTRUCTIONAL POINTERS ••••••••

1. *Clients are generally more comfortable if their arms are in a vertical position, or one in which they can rest on the supporting environment.*

2. *Mention, on one or two occassions in the wording, not to put too much pressure on the finger tips.*

3. *When debriefing allow clients to share what happened spontaneously during the technique.*

THE SEQUENCE OF SENSORY AWARENESS TECHNIQUES

There is no prescribed sequence of sensory awareness training techniques. However, techniques which narrow the focus of attention to one or two sensations initially may be the most beneficial to the client. The partner sensory awareness technique serves well as the initial training technique. Although each individual is perceiving and experiencing sensations within his/her body, the partner is assisting in the formulation of the sensations.

The partner sensory awareness technique is an excellent starting point, too, because all clients can perceive and experience something. This success encourages clients to continue their efforts to feel other sensations throughout the body. For most it is a time of discovery, a time in which they are intrigued with the findings. Actually, the sensations and perceptions discovered have been there all along but now the client can experience them on a more conscious level.

Client responses to partner sensory awareness which reinforce its use as a beginning technique include:

It is a safe way of being touched, thus reducing boundaries between individuals.

It is an easy way to begin focusing within one's body where one can notice a calming effect without actually peforming a relaxation technique.

It reduces some of the skepticism regarding relaxation techniques.

It fosters trust in the relationship between the client and the facilitator, and in oneself to let go and just experience.

Following the partner sensory awareness technique, the facilitator can focus on techniques for either the upper body (e.g., fingertips, hand clench, etc.) or the lower body (e.g., the stand). As clients develop keener observation skills in selected body areas, the facilitator can present techniques designed for the entire body (e.g., body search).[4]

The body search technique focuses predominantly on internal sensations. It is helpful for clients to sense and feel movement or tension while mentally scanning the body. Then clients should scan for and focus on stillness; that is, some area in the body where there is no perceived movement or tension. In both the movement and stillness phases, the client feels, senses, and experiences only what is being perceived.

These techniques lay an excellent foundation for relaxation training. The abilities to perceive and to experience sensations are both preliminary steps to relaxation and integral to many specific relaxation techniques. Thus, sensory awareness training is an important part of a relaxation program.

•••••••••INSTRUCTIONAL POINTERS•••••••••

The role of the relaxation facilitator is to guide or ease client learning. To enhance the learning of sensory awareness skills, the facilitator should:

1. Become familiar with the diverse sensory aware-ness techniques prior to guiding clients through them.

2. Use words like "allow," "permit," "sense," "feel," "experience," "notice," or "discover" to evoke perceptions of facts, processes, or reactions within the body. (See Chapter 3 for further discussion on wording.)

3. Indicate sensory awareness is not a relaxation technique even though most clients will report they feel relaxed.

4. Allow ample opportunities for clients to share their perceived sensations with the group or facilitator. This often assists other clients to recall a similar sensation. It further reinforces that every person may feel something different.

5. Keep the focus on experiencing sensations rather than judging or searching for the cause. Non-judgmental conscious awareness is the first step in changing habits or patterns of reacting to the environment.

6. Present techniques in a slow, rhythmic, and deliberate manner. Enough time should be provided between parts of the techniques to allow clients time to note sensations.

7. Use the compare-contrast approach of body parts or opposite sensations to assist the client in the discovery and learning process.

CHAPTER 8

THE BREATHING RHYTHM

THE BREATHING RHYTHM IN RELAXATION TRAINING

Breathing, one of the major physiological activities which sustains life, is regulated spontaneously by the diaphragm. Breathing also can be consciously regulated. The diaphragm is a dome-shaped, musculomembranous wall which separates the abdomen from the thoracic cavity. During the inhalation phase of breathing, the chest cavity is expanded as the diaphragm moves downward and the muscles of the chest wall pull the ribs outward allowing air to be drawn into the lungs. As the diaphragm moves upward and the chest muscles relax causing the rib cage to become smaller, air is expelled. This is the exhalation phase of breathing. In a total breathing cycle there are two more phases. A pause exists between the inhalation and the exhalation phases. When this pause becomes exaggerated at the end of the inhalation, as in a sudden start or various athletic endeavors, it is a holding of the breath.

Physical, physiological actions, feelings, and images are associated with each of these breathing phases. Paying attention to the breathing rhythm and practicing breathing techniques is useful for (1) discovering a personal breathing rhythm where the breathing apparatus moves freely, (2) a preventive or ameliorative strategy for managing stress, i.e., eliciting the relaxation response, (3) enhancing mental acuity, stimulation, or power for athletes, dancers, business persons, actors and other professionals, and (4) therapeutic procedures whereby a trained therapist assists the client in managing a specific health problem. In this book the focus will be how to use the breathing phases for relaxation, invigoration and stimulation, and how one can use the imagination positively.

EXHALATION AND RELAXATION

If you can breathe, you can relax. The body's built-in relaxation mechanism, the exhalation phase of the breathing cycle, contains the explanation for such a statement. By paying attention to exhalations there is a spontaneous letting go of tension developed during the inhalation breath. A number of sensations, all of which are associated with relaxation, accompany this letting go. Many of the sensations perceived by clients are noted in Table 8-1.

Table 8 - 1

Sensations Related to Exhalations

Heaviness
Sinking down; descending; falling asleep
Warmth
Slowing down; patience
Boredom
Relaxed feeling; letting go; release of tension
Lengthening of breathing
Comfort; contentment

Taken from J. Curtis & R. Detert,
  How To Relax: A Holistic Approach To Stress Management
  (Palo Alto, CA: Mayfield Publishing Company, 1981), p. 85.

Adapted from Beata Jencks, *Your Body: Biofeedback at Its Best*
  (Chicago: Nelson Hall, 1977), pp. 136-137.

To begin instruction, the facilitator has clients focus on the exhalation while passively disregarding the inhalation. The facilitator then asks clients to select one sensation associated with the exhalation phase of breathing and to focus on this sensation in the same way as in sensory awareness training. Since sensations of heaviness or sinking down are the easiest to perceive, the facilitator may begin by selecting one of these and having clients focus on perceiving heaviness or sinking down. Normally, by focusing on the sensation in time with each exhalation, a person can begin to feel relaxed in three to four guided breaths.

Following these initial guided breaths, clients begin to establish a personal breathing rhythm. With continued focus on exhalations, breathing automatically will become slower and deeper. The face, throat, and shoulder muscles will become more relaxed. Clients may perceive being breathed rather than consciously, actively breathing. Once familiar with the variety of sensations associated with exhalation and relaxation, it is possible for the facilitator to guide clients into a more deeply relaxed state.

Sample Exhalation Technique

The relaxation facilitator can enhance the guiding of clients in breathing techniques by knowing how and why the techniques are presented to the clients. Table 8-2 presents one such technique. The left portion of the table describes the technique used in guiding the client. The right side is a brief explanation for its inclusion in the technique.

Table 8 - 2

Exhalation Technique

Technique Description	Rationale
1. Sit upright in a chair with the eyes closed.	1. A basic relaxation position
2. Breathe normally while focusing your attention on your breathing rhythm. Listen to yourself breathe for three or four breathing cycles.	2. Passive focusing on breathing rhythm in general
3. After listening for three or four cycles, focus your attention inward and concentrate on the exhalation phase of the breathing rhythm and the sensation you would like to observe.	3. Guided focus of exhalation with a sensation associated with relaxation
4. Focus on the sensation only during the exhalation phase of the breathing rhythm. Do not think about the inhalation at all - just allow your body to inhale when it desires.	4. Passive disregard of inhalation. Allowing the person to establish personal breathing rhythm.
5. Do not prolong the exhalations - just allow the body to breathe.	5. Suggestion of not consciously changing breathing rhythm. Allowing oneself to "be breathed" by the body.
6. Example: Each time you exhale, feel the heaviness as you are breathing out. Allow your mind to go blank during the inhalations. Feel the heaviness again as you exhale. You may feel this heaviness in the head, the neck, the trunk, arms, hands, fingers, legs, buttocks, feet, or throughout the entire body. Just feel the heaviness somewhere as you exhale. Focus within the body and allow the heaviness to happen.	6. Sensory awareness of sensations associated with relaxation and properly timed with personal exhalation rate
7. After you feel and experience heaviness during the exhalation phase for several breathing cycles, terminate the exercise by flexing, stretching, taking a deep breath, and opening your eyes.	7. Proper termination of exercise to gradually allow person to return to awake state.

Taken from J. Curtis and R. Detert, *How To Relax: A Holistic Approach To Stress Management* (Palo Alto, CA: Mayfield Publishing Company, 1981), pp. 85-86.

• • • • • • • • • INSTRUCTIONAL POINTER • • • • • • • •

A general rule of voice control here is to speak at normal volume and lower the voice as you continue to have clients focus on exhalations; speak at normal volume during inhalation exercises and raise voice slightly when terminating the technique.

Although this technique will induce a relaxed state, it is not intended to be used as a relaxation technique by itself. It is included in a total relaxation program as a foundation exercise for (1) reinforcing sensory awareness training, (2) focusing on the exhalation phase of the breathing cycle where relaxation can be achieved, and (3) introducing the notion of passive expectancy coupled with a specific phase of the breathing cycle. Later, in each relaxation technique clients tune into the exhalation phase for several breathing cycles as a preliminary step to the technique itself.

INHALATION AND INVIGORATION

As inhaled air moves downward into the lungs, the body moves upward. Inhalation is invigorating, strengthening, exhilarating; it also produces tension. The inhalation phase of the breathing cycle is used mainly (1) to terminate relaxation techniques, and (2) in conjunction with certain imagination techniques. The latter will be described in more detail in Chapter 11.

As a foundation technique, inhalation techniques assist clients to develop a keener awareness of the physical or psychological sensations or actions associated with invigoration and tension. Many of these sensations can be noted in Table 8-3.

Table 8 - 3

Inhalation Sensations

Invigoration
Increased tension
Coolness
Hardness
Dryness
Expansion (chest region)
Tightening
Upward body movement; ascending; levitating
Alertness; awakening
Gasping; speeding; being startled
Refreshment
Preparation for action

> Taken from J. Curtis & R. Detert,
> *How To Relax: A Holistic Approach to Stress Management*
> (Palo Alto, CA: Mayfield Publishing Company, 1981) p. 83.
>
> Adapted from Beata Jencks, *Your Body: Biofeedback at Its Best*
> (Chicago: Nelson Hall, 1977), pp. 136-137.

Clients report increased tension of chest muscles, rising of the shoulders, and coolness of the air as it moves into the nostrils as the easiest to sense. The facilitator guides clients through the inhalation technique in much the same way as the exhalation technique. However, the facilitator should not prolong the inhalation technique. Clients tend to breathe in harder and deeper when attempting to perceive these sensations. During inhalation, clients are actually trying to feel the sensations rather than allowing them to occur as in exhalation. Trying too hard may bring on hyperventilation. To prevent hyperventilation keep the technique short.

Sample Inhalation Technique

Table 8-4 presents a simple inhalation technique with accompanying rationale. The inhalation technique assists clients in perceiving sensations or actions that are different from the exhalation sensations. Although many of the sensations or actions are opposites, this is not necessarily true for all sensations. Being able to note the different sensations is important for clients when using the inhalation technique with the imagination techniques presented later in this book.

Table 8 - 4

Inhalation Technique

Technique Description	Rationale
1. Sit upright in a chair with your eyes closed.	1. A basic relaxation position.
2. Take a breath as you concentrate on the inhalation phase and the sensation you want to observe.	2. Guided focus of inhalation with a sensation associated with tension, invigoration, etc.
3. Exhale, but do not think about the exhalation. Simply allow your body to exhale on its own accord.	3. Passive disregard of exhalation and allowing the body to breathe at its own rate.
4. Focus all of your attention on the inhalation phase. Repeat the inhalation three to four times, concentrating and feeling any of the sensations listed in Table 8 - 3. Again, disregard the exhalations.	4. Focus on inhalation for specific sensation(s).
5. Let yourself experience each feeling, action, or image for several breaths.	5. Experiencing the sensation in time with inhalations and gaining control of this phase of breathing cycle.
6. Flex-stretch-inhale, and open your eyes.	6. Proper termination of exercise.

Taken from J. Curtis and R. Detert, *How To Relax: A Holistic Approach To Stress Managment* (Palo Alto, CA: Mayfield Publishing Company, 1981), pp. 83-84.

• • • • • • • • • INSTRUCTIONAL POINTERS • • • • • • • •

1. Review instructional pointers for sensory awareness training since they apply here as well.

2. To alleviate some client fears, discuss the various phases of the breathing cycle prior to guiding clients in the technique. Some clients have reported negative experiences with their breathing in other relaxation classes or due to a health problem. It may be important to move very slowly with these individuals and allow them to perform as much of the technique as they are comfortable performing. It has been our experience that these individuals will be able to perform all the techniques if given time and encouragement.

3. Some individuals may have learned breathing methods which are different from those presented here. Encourage clients to try these techniques. Ultimately clients should use techniques that result in the most success.

4. Begin with the exhalation technique and the sensations of heaviness or sinking down because they are the easiest sensations for clients to perceive.

5. If guiding more than one client at a time, the facilitator may find it helpful to time the technique phrases with just one client. Encourage clients to perceive sensations in time with their own breathing since you cannot stay in time with all of them. Many facilitators prefer to guide according to their personal breathing rhythm allowing clients to gauge their breathing accordingly. However, when first teaching a class many facilitators feel somewhat stressed and may be breathing too rapidly for the majority of participants.

6. Forced changes in rate and depth of breathing from trying too hard can lead to hyperventilation. If clients mention light-headedness, dizziness, ringing or buzzing in the ears, or a trembling feeling, discontinue the technique. The facilitator should continually encourage clients to breathe normally at all times. Clients do not need to consciously change breathing patterns in order to focus on a breathing phase or sensation. Also the facilitator should not prolong any breathing technique until it is ascertained that all clients are comfortable with their breathing pattern.

CHAPTER 9

SUPPORTING ENVIRONMENT TECHNIQUES

To perform any relaxation technique, there must be something under the body to support it. Any surface, where the pull of gravity can be sensed, that offers support to the various body parts (head, arms, legs, buttocks) or the body as a whole becomes the supporting environment. Chairs, couches, beds and even the floor, when one is standing on it, are examples of the supporting environment. Since relaxation techniques are performed on supporting environments, the facilitator should provide useful instruction in how clients can use this support for relaxation or other special purposes.

As an introduction, the facilitator can discuss a number of sensations clients may perceive while performing a supporting environment technique. Most common sensations are a letting go or release of muscular tension, descending or sinking down, heaviness, comfort and security, and a blending of body parts with the supporting surface. Techniques can be developed by the facilitator to have clients sense specific certain sensations. As with the breathing rhythm techniques, the supporting environment techniques continue to enhance the development of sensory awareness capabilities.

Sensory awareness is enhanced as the facilitator guides the client through the technique by having the client note: the presence of body parts against the chair or floor; various body parts which seem to be in contact with the supporting surface; a blending of body parts with the surface; body or body parts as distinct from, yet a part of, the support surface; heaviness or sinking as one experiences the pull of gravity; and focusing on muscular tension flowing out of the body into the supporting surface. When guiding clients in supporting environment techniques, the facilitator should provide sufficient time for the client to develop a conscious acceptance of the supporting surface and a sense of security and contentment. The letting go so often mentioned in relaxation thus becomes not solely a freeing up of the mental processes but further a giving up of the body to the supporting surface.

SAMPLE SUPPORTING ENVIRONMENT TECHNIQUES

The hand and the body techniques serve different purposes. The hand technique in Table 9-1 was developed for clients to experience either a giving up or a blending of the fingers and hands with the supporting surface. On a larger scale, the body technique in Table 9-2 was designed to have clients note where a body part is in contact with the supporting surface and, while exhaling, allow the surface to support that area of the body. All major contact points are covered in this technique which allows clients to experience release of tension, achieve a sense of security, and note other sensory sensations.

Table 9 - 1

Supporting Environment Technique: The Hand

Technique Description	Rationale
1. Assume the desired relaxation position with your hands rotated so your fingers are in contact with the supporting surface.	1. Basic relaxation position and position of hands.
2. When ready, exhale and allow your eyes to close. Focus on your exhalations for several more breathing cycles.	2. Guided focus on relaxation phase of breathing cycle.
3. Turn your attention to your right thumb. Focus now on the exact spot where your thumb and supporting surface meet and for several exhalations, allow the thumb to become part of the supporting surface.	3. Focus on initial selected body part (hand) / blending (giving up) of part to support surface.
4. Next, turn your attention to your index finger, the exact place where it meets the supporting surface. On the next two exhalations, allow that finger to become part of the supporting surface. On the third exhalation, focus on both the thumb and index finger and allow both to be totally supported by the supporting surface.	4. Focus on second selected body part (index finger) / blending of part to support surface/giving up first and second selected parts to the support surface.
5. Proceed in the same manner until all fingers and thumb of the right hand have been focused upon. Then focus on entire hand and, for 2 or 3 exhalations, allow the hand to be supported by the supporting environment.	5. Focus on third, fourth, and fifth body parts (middle finger, ring finger, little finger)/blending of *each* part to support surface/giving up of selected parts 1 & 2 & 3, etc., to support surface/allowing whole hand to be totally supported by support surface.
6. Repeat with left thumb, fingers, and hand.	6. Same as with right hand.
7. Focus now on both hands as they are totally supported by the supporting surface. Feel and experience how comfortable your hands have become. Notice which parts of your hands are partially in contact with the supporting environment.	7. Giving up of both hands to support surface/sensory awareness of sensations which may now be perceived by client, including relaxation.
8. When ready, flex-stretch-inhale and open your eyes.	8. Termination of exercise.

Table 9 - 2

Supporting Environment Technique: The Body

Technique Description	Rationale
1. Assume the desired supine position with your arms resting comfortably at your sides.	1. Basic relaxation position.
2. Tune into your exhalations, listen to yourself breathe for several breaths, and r-e-l-a-x as you exhale.	2. Guided focus on relaxation phase of breathing cycle.
3. Now focus your attention to the back of your heels where they are in contact with the floor. For 2 or 3 exhalations, allow the floor to support this area of your feet as they become slightly heavy and sink into the supporting surface.	3. Focus on body parts in contact with supporting environment/allowing support surface to support body parts/sensory awareness of heaviness of limbs or other feelings, emotions, sensations.
4. Turn attention to each selected body area, one at a time. With each area, spend 2 or 3 exhalations while giving up that area to be supported by the supporting environment. Suggested body areas include calves, buttocks, upper back and shoulders, upper arms, forearms, palms and fingers, back of head.	4. Continuation of point three above.
5. For the next three to four breaths, focus on your entire body. Allow it to be totally supported by the supporting environment. Feel your arms and legs becoming comfortably heavy, your entire body relax, the letting go of muscular tension.	5. Letting go of muscular tension - giving entire body up to supporting surface/sensory awareness of contentment or security as release of tension and relaxation occurs.
6. As your entire body is supported by the supporting environment, notice there is minimal muscular tension throughout your body and notice also the contentment, the secure feeling you have as you allow the supporting environment to support your entire body.	6. Gaining confidence in letting go.
7. Wait for two or three more breathing cycles and then flex, stretch, take a deep breath, and open your eyes.	7. Termination of exercise.

•••••••••INSTRUCTIONAL POINTERS•••••••••

1.   *In order to develop or guide clients in supporting environment techniques, the facilitator should be familiar with four major areas of the body. These areas are: lower legs (feet, ankles, calves); upper legs and buttocks (thighs and buttocks); upper body (trunk, shoulders, head and neck); arms (upper arms, lower arms, hands and fingers).*[1]

2.   *The facilitator should be aware that some individuals have a great deal of difficulty, or an actual fear of, letting go. They want to remain in charge, to be in control of every thing that happens to them. For them, letting go is a major source of stress. To avoid potential problems and alleviate the fear of letting go, the facilitator could use the sequence of foundation techniques mentioned in the next pointer.*

3.   *Although a supporting environment technique can be used to guide a client into relaxation, it is generally intended as a foundation for relaxation techniques. The facilitator may best serve clients if the supporting environment techniques include: the basic position, focusing on the exhalation phase of breathing; perceiving sensory sensations; and the supporting environment. When guiding clients in a total body relaxation technique, each of these components should be reduced to one or two sentences as preliminary to the actual relaxation phrases. Thus, conditioning and training for each area are essential.*

4.   *With proper guidance and practice, clients can achieve minimum muscular tension and letting go through the supporting environment technique. The* facilitator can enhance the release of muscular tension by checking body position for proper alignment, i.e., good alignment of limbs, torso, and head.

5. Since an altered state of consciousness may develop with a supporting environment technique, have clients remain in their position for several breathing cycles following the technique to avoid light headedness, dizziness, and/or fainting.

6. The facilitator should lead a short discussion session following each technique to allow clients to share the sensations noted and success or difficulties in performing the technique.

7. With some groups, the jargon may get in the way of enhancing relaxation. If the words "supporting environment" are actually built into the phrasing of the technique, let clients know in advance what this means. Clients will then be able to interpret the term to mean floor, chair, etc. When guiding the client, use the actual word of chair, floor, or bed in place of supporting environment. Use whatever seems to be less confusing to clients so they won't have to work mentally to understand the words.

CHAPTER 10

PHYSIOLOGICAL PATHWAYS OF STRESS AND RELAXATION

Individuals involved in the control and amelioration of stress are very much aware of the vast number of strategies from which to choose. Like stress management strategies in general, relaxation training encompasses a variety of skills and approaches. Most relaxation training strategies seem to have as a goal to (1) reduce the intensity of physical arousal from stress, (2) offset and reduce the chemical by-products of the stress response, (3) retrain mind-body pathways for better harmonious functioning, or (4) a combination of the first three. Whatever the goal, and whether it be for educational purposes of the healthy population or for therapeutic purposes with those who have sought a health care provider, the relaxation facilitator has an arsenal of techniques to use with clients.

In addition to the variety of methods discussed in this text, the facilitator can further draw from yoga, hypnosis with suggested relaxation, and many more. A skilled stress management facilitator should be familiar and competent with a number of psychophysiological methods to maximize success with clients. Although a client can usually receive benefit from any one specific technique, one specific technique may not be suitable for every person. What works on one day for an individual may not be successful on another day with the same person. What works in the general control of stress during the day or as a transition from work to leisure may not work to foster sleep. An explanation of what occurs in some of the stress and relaxation pathways of the body will serve to illustrate the need to know many relaxation techniques.

BASIC STRESS AND TENSION PATHWAYS

The stress pathways of the mind-body relationship involve complex neurophysiological processes. It is not the purpose of this manual to describe in detail the endocrine and nervous system processes but, rather, to illustrate some basic concepts of neurophysiological processing systems to show how relaxation training works and why competence in several techniques is most helpful for the client.

FUNCTIONAL PHYSIOLOGY

CENTRAL NERVOUS SYSTEM

Examine for a moment Figure 10-1. The central nervous system (CNS) consists of the brain and spinal cord. The brain can be subdivided into three fundamental levels: (1) the brainstem, (2) the limbic system, and (3) the neocortex.

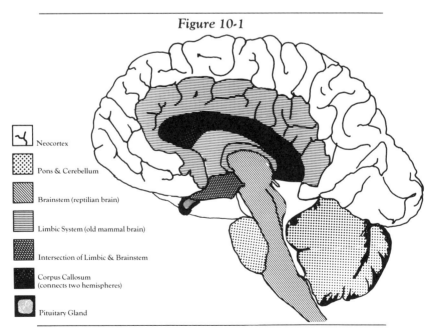

Figure 10-1

Neocortex

Pons & Cerebellum

Brainstem (reptilian brain)

Limbic System (old mammal brain)

Intersection of Limbic & Brainstem

Corpus Callosum
(connects two hemispheres)

Pituitary Gland

The brainstem, composed of the medulla oblongata, thalamus, and hypothalamus, functions to maintain the body's healthy status even during relaxing and stressful times. During rest or exercise, for example, nerve centers in the brainstem control respiration and heart rate, adjusting them to respond to oxygen and blood needs of body tissues. Intense tickling in the nose can signal a nerve center in the brainstem to create a sneeze, thus allowing the body to protect itself from foreign material.

The limbic system is believed to be the seat of emotional response to the internal and external environments. The Papez-Maclean theory of brain function[1] suggests that emotional overrides to the basic functioning of the brainstem allowed primitive species of mammals to compete more successfully and survive the rigors of nature. Emotions exemplified by sexual drives, feelings of anger and frustration, the paternal/maternal affection for offspring, and sensations of pleasure and anxiety allowed our early ancestors to respond with greater specificity to environmental challenges, insuring survival to more of their offspring. The physiological process of running away from or fighting a man-eating creature was no longer the necessary condition to elicit an increase in heart rate, blood pressure, and respiration rate from the brainstem. The sight of the man-eating creature could now evoke from an emotional memory the past experiences of horror and create the current experience of fear. The experience of fear itself could increase heart rate, blood pressure, and respiration rate thus preparing the body for the physiological process of running away or fighting. Emotions thus became a method for enhancing the specificity of responses to the environment. Emotions can, and do, elicit physiological changes within the body, whether emotions of anxiety and anger or of joy and affection.

The neocortex — as exemplified in man — allowed thought processes in the brain to reach an abstract and symbolic level language and writing. Thinking with what-if's and if then's provided even more control over the environment and provided man with the potential to plan for future events. The neocortex provided modifications and fine tunings to the basic emotions expressed in the limbic system, creating more abstract emotions like platonic love (agape) and greed.

It is easy to see that all three of these basic brain levels are associated with the psychological or physiological responses to stressors. Since the three levels are neuronally interlinked, abstract thoughts or emotions from the neocortex can have an impact upon the limbic system, which in turn can alter basic body physiology controlled by the brainstem. The body can, and does, react physiologically to thoughts and emotions as if they were real. This important point demonstrates why positive and calming thoughts and emotions can also have a beneficial impact during the relaxation process.

RETICULAR ACTIVATING SYSTEM

There is one major neuronal pathway which strongly interconnects all three levels of the brain. This neuronal pathway, the Reticular Activating System (R.A.S. for short), plays an important role in priming the cortex to receive important information coming in from sensory neurons throughout the body. A dulled R.A.S. (due to alcohol consumption) would perform a poorer job of preparing the cortex to receive and process information while a hypersensitized R.A.S. (due to LSD use) could create an alert, ready cortex that interprets low level sensory stimuli as high level, major messages. (This is one theory about why LSD use enhances the senses.) The R.A.S. also modulates outgoing motor impulses to the body.

The level of activity of the R.A.S. reflects the level of arousal of the individual. An alert, even anxious, individual would have an active R.A.S., but an individual who is relaxed and calm would have a less active R.A.S. An individual who is asleep has an even quieter R.A.S. (except for dreaming).

Even though it may not be consciously perceived, when a person encounters stress he or she stimulates body physiology through the process described above. These increased body functions send an increased level of sensory information to the R.A.S., which then sends this increased level of sensory information to the cortex for subliminal or liminal interpretation and further processing. Since one of the capabilities of the neocortex is to alter the functioning of the R.A.S., the cortex, if the information is interpreted as important, dangerous, or valuable, can increase the sensitivity of the R.A.S. to further incoming sensory information. Perhaps an example would be beneficial. If a client is worried about tension headaches created by neck and shoulder tension, this worry can bring about a tension headache. At a homeostatic condition, the muscles send impulses back to the brain regarding the amount of muscle tone and tension in the muscle fibers. If the individual perceives this information with anxiety (through the intellectual process of the cortex) the cortex may sensitize the R.A.S. to further sensory information from the muscle fibers. But instead of a negative feedback process, the individual may respond to the anxiety by further tensing muscle fibers. A stimulated R.A.S. may also sensitize the interpreting cortex to other body sensations, and, depending on the interpretation of these incoming sensory stimuli, may provide feedback for the individual to control body physiology (as in biofeedback) or create an anxiety-filled situation in which the client further tightens muscles, increases heart rate and blood pressure, and more.

Impulses in the R.A.S. have the capacity for prolonging a response to a stimulus. When stressors are encountered in rapid succession, the R.A.S. may reverberate impulses from the first stressful encounter, providing a carry-over effect to the next stressor. The R.A.S. can accumulate the sensory impulses from the succession of stressors and become highly active. In speaking about this capacity for reverberation, Girdano and Everly have stated:

> The R.A.S. has the capacity for reverberation (prolonged vibration) of an impulse and will also prolong a response. This means that the R.A.S. can maintain a resting level of activity which is reflective of the general state of the other brain structures. A high level of resting activity inhibits and shortens potential arousal. If you live a stressful life and find that you are stressed many times during the day, chances are that the parts of the brain that become aroused to deal with that stress also affect the R.A.S., which adapts to frequent arousal by staying aroused. It is as if the R.A.S. is saying, "Well, if you are going to be aroused so often I might as well just stay aroused and save the time and energy of going up and down." The R.A.S. also has the capacity to recruit impulses from other brain structures and it will adapt to stimuli. It is partly because of this ability to adapt that repeated situations cause less stress than novel experiences and the noise of the city is less stressful for the permanent resident than for the visitor.[2]

Once the R.A.S. becomes over-stimulated from encounters with stress, mental and physical activities accelerate. The body feeds the mind, the mind feeds the body, with the R.A.S. serving as an important link. This not only explains conditions of stress, but also conditions of relaxation.

AUTONOMIC NERVOUS SYSTEM

The central nervous system is only one portion of the total neural network of the body. All nerves that are not a part of the central nervous system are collectively called the peripheral nervous system. These nerves extend from the central nervous system and innervate the body organs, muscles, glands, and skin. The peripheral nervous system can be further subdivided into the voluntary motor system and the autonomic nervous system. The voluntary motor system innervates the muscles, predominantly, and is the neural network that allows the brain to create voluntary motion - like picking up a glass, or painting a work of art. The autonomic nervous system innervates organs, glands, and the skin, and used to be considered out of the realm of voluntary control, hence the title autonomic. Early research in biofeedback dispelled this concept and we now know that individuals can learn to control portions of their autonomic nervous system. This point is very relevant because many of the physiological effects of stress manifest themselves through the autonomic nervous system. The racing heart, the sweaty palms, the increase in blood pressure are all effects of the autonomic nervous system. But the effects of relaxation also manifest themselves through the autonomic nervous system! To understand this point it is necessary to take a look at further subdivisions of the autonomic nervous system.

Sympathetic and Parasympathetic Nervous Systems

The autonomic nervous system can be subdivided conceptually into two pathways: the sympathetic and parasympathetic nervous systems. Besides using different neurotransmitters and innervating organs in slightly different ways, the two systems look very similar. Their effects, however, are almost opposite. The sympathetic nervous system has been conceptually considered the *fight or flight* system of the body and, when stimulated, elicits physiological changes necessary for extreme physical exertion and confrontation. The parasympathetic nervous system has been conceptually considered the *rest and repose* system of the body and, when stimulated, allows the body to conserve energy and digest and store foodstuffs.

Both of these branches of the autonomic nervous system continually send neural impulses to the target organs they innervate, creating a baseline amount of stimulation called neural tone. This neural tone provides more regulatory control of target organs within the body because an increase or decrease in neural tone can alter in small amounts the stimulation to the target organ. If the sympathetic or parasympathetic nervous systems only sent impulses at particular times, and did not send impulses at other times, target organs could only be stimulated or not stimulated. Thus, neural tone provides more discriminatory control of the body.

Under stressful conditions, the neural tone of the sympathetic nervous system pathway is increased while the tone of the parasympathetic pathway may be unchanged or decreased. The increased tone in the sympathetic nervous system elicits the fight or flight response typically experienced in emergency or life-threatening situations, but minor stressors may also elicit a more minor increase in sympathetic tone and its consequent symptomology.

Under more relaxing conditions, such as during stress management training, the neural tone of the parasysmpathetic system is increased while the tone of the sympathetic system is decreased. This results in the rest and repose response (or relaxation response). Current research has indicated that the "relaxation response" may be generated more from the reduction in sympathetic nervous system tone than the increase in parasympathetic nervous system tone.[3] Body physiology alters during the "relaxation response" so that heart rate and cardiac output decrease, the skin becomes less sweaty, blood becomes shunted to the digestive system, and more.

RELAXATION: THEORY AND PRACTICE

Both the stress response and the relaxation response function through the neural pathways described above. Through a training process involving relaxation exercises, the client may regulate a balance in these pathways, thus affecting the body's physiology.

Psychophysiological methods of relaxation imply that both the mind and the body are involved in the quieting process. Although the points of focus for relaxation training may vary with the technique selected, eventually the higher and lower levels of the neural pathways become involved. For example, the point of focus for Progressive Relaxation Training is in the various muscle groups of the body. As the client focuses attention on muscle groups and allows them to relax, the R.A.S., cortex, and other brain regions sense the decreased muscular activity and tension. Fewer impulses reaching the R.A.S. and cortex allow both structures to reach a lower level of stimulation and modify, therefore, stimulation to other brain regions and stimulation to body organs via the neural pathways. With this modification of incoming and outgoing neural impulses comes the benefits associated with relaxation.

The focus of relaxation techniques like Benson's Relaxation Response, meditation, and hypnosis with suggested relaxation is in the thought processes within the cortex. Through mental processes, extraneous thoughts and stimuli are reduced or controlled. The resultant changes in cortical activity can modify the R.A.S. and other brain regions so that the physiological correlates of relaxation occur within the whole body.

Other techniques, Bezzola's Autoanalysis, Schultz's Standard Autogenic Training, Sensory Awareness Training, and Jencks Respiration for Special Accomplishment usually involve the cortex, the skeletal muscles, and internal organs or systems. It is difficult to isolate a true focus with these exercises. It may be best to state that these techniques attempt to focus on both the mental processes and the body symptomology.

One way to categorize relaxation techniques can be based upon the initial focus of the technique. Those techniques that first attempt to modify body symptomology (e.g., tense muscles) and have as an end result the relaxation of the cognitive processes can be labelled somatopsychic relaxation techniques. Those relaxation techniques that first attempt to modify the cognitive processes of the mind (e.g., excessive rumination or anxiety) and that have as an end result the relaxation of the body physiology can be labelled psychosomatic relaxation techniques. Note, however, that some relaxation techniques defy this simple classification scheme and may be considered in both categories.

The relaxation facilitator, therefore, should be competent in both psychosomatic relaxation techniques as well as somato-psychic techniques. By assessing whether the source of the stress is predominantly cognitive (overstimulation of mental processes) or somatic (tension in muscles or other stress symptomology) the facilitator can proceed to experiment with the appropriate technique or combination of techniques for maximum benefit. Some clients may find psychosomatic techniques difficult and somatopsychic techniques easy, or vice versa. This information helps the facilitator select from the many relaxation techniques available and makes the matching process between client and relaxation technique easier.

The variety of approaches the facilitator uses can further stimulate and motivate the client to continue using and experimenting with techniques. Of course, the facilitator and the client need to keep in mind that success comes with continual practice; experimentation should conclude with a regimen that the client can use in a practical, efficient way.

CHAPTER 11

USE OF VISUALIZATION IN RELAXATION TRAINING

The use of visualization techniques as one component of a holistic relaxation program has grown greatly during the last decade. When instructed and facilitated properly, visualization techniques provide an exciting approach for inducing healthy psychological and physical reactions useful in preventing unnecessary stress or in ameliorating harmful outcomes from too much stress. Visualization techniques currently are being used successfully in the treatment of various illnesses.

Drs. Carl and Stephanie Matthews-Simonton have used *healing visualization* as an adjunct approach to cancer therapy. They have their clients mentally picture the effect traditional cancer therapy has on the disease process. Their approach involves changing attitudes which can have a pronounced impact on the physical outcome of the disease process.[1,2,3,4]

Using visualization exercises, or *active imagination,* is also part of the work of Dr. Gerry Jampolsky. At the Center for Attitudinal Healing in Tiburon, California, Dr. Jampolsky assists young persons experiencing physical or emotional pain associated with a catastrophic illness by using imagery to replace negative thoughts with positive ones. His goal is to have clients experience moments of health derived from inner peace, letting go of fear, forgiving, and loving.[5,6]

Another application of imagery is that used by Dr. Beata Jencks. With imagined breathing pathways, Dr. Jencks has developed imagery exercises which can be used for pain control, reduction of muscular tension, relief of tension headaches, opening congested sinuses, maintaining a healthy psychophysiological balance within the body and other specific health accomplishments.[7,8]

Examples of how the imagination is employed for the prevention or the amelioration of harmful health conditions are endless. Some of the approaches are questionable to the scientific community, while others are on the cutting edge of harnessing the mind's tremendous healing and restorative powers. We present these examples, without judgment as to their effectiveness or acceptance by the medical or lay community, to inform the reader of what is being done to capture and promote the mind's energy for more positive uses.

The purpose of this chapter, however, is to explore the use of visualization techniques for self-training or group instruction with the educational focus of knowledge and skill development. Each of these techniques can be adapted by the professional therapist for use in physical therapy, occupational therapy, psychotherapy, and other health related professions.

THE CONSCIOUS AND SUBCONSCIOUS MIND

Visualization techniques involve using the mind, thus the imagination. The mind has both conscious and subconscious properties. Since the subconscious properties require special training to examine the interaction of sensations, thought and will with emotions, impulses and desires, that will not be discussed in any detail here. Germane to this discussion is how to acquire a more healthy control of the conscious mind.

The conscious mind includes the properties of perception, memory, thinking, emotions, and will.[9] Each of these properties interacts with the subconsious mind and has done so since birth. One cannot directly control the subconsious mind but, to a large degree, one can give increased positive attention to (1) life events or other ongoing processes through the senses (our perceptions), and (2) thought processes, including those leading to self-talk and self-concept, and the intensity of the emotions of anger, guilt, disgust, fear, grief, joy and surprise.

Giving positive attention to the properties of the conscious mind via visualization techniques, an individual can begin to consciously disregard how things affected one in the past and replace them with new experiences. These new experiences create new memories for more immediate use. If a person thinks or imagines pleasant, relaxing and tranquil thoughts, with practice the body will physiologically respond to produce a relaxed state.

TERMINOLOGY

Several terms are often used interchangeably when discussing the use of visualization. To avoid semantic confusion when teaching classes or working with clients, Jencks offers the following descriptions:

Image: A central nervous system-aroused mental representation, not necessarily visual, of sensations or perceptions or reproduction or reconstruction of perceptual experiences in the apparent absence of sensory stimulation.

Imagery: The collective term for images and the operation of forming images in perception, thought, feeling, memory and fantasy in the apparent absence of sensory stimulation.

Imagination: The formulation of ideas, pictures, emotions, sensory perceptions and sensations of physical activity in the mind from memories or purely by invention. Simplest to imagine are objects, places or feelings followed by actions such as walking, sitting or sleeping.

Visualization Techniques: Techniques which employ conscious, intentional imagery, and make use of self-suggestions for psychological or physiological purposes. One does not actually have to view a scene to successfully use these techniques.[10]

TYPES OF IMAGES

An individual can experience several types of images (see Table 11-1). These images can occur in any sense modality. Most frequently employed sense modalities used in assisting image formation include visual (seeing images on one's mental screen), auditory (hearing sounds associated with the image), olfactory (perceiving smells associated with a scene), gustatory (perception of taste associated with image formation), tactile (stimulus leading to the perceptions of touch, pressure, heat, cold and pain), and kinesthesis (passively or actively produced discrimination of positions and movements of body parts based on information other than visual or auditory; this stimuli arises from tension, compression, pull of gravity, and muscular contraction).[11]

Thus, visualization techniques can be effective even if clients are unable to produce a visual image. Faint, subjective representation of a thought or action engages the mental process of the brain. In turn, there is interaction with corresponding neural and hormonal pathways.

Each type of imagery may occur separately or in combinations. However, most individuals are able to evoke some type of image. Regardless of age, practice can increase one's ability to evoke this imagery.

ABILITY TO EVOKE IMAGERY

Everyone has some innate capacity to evoke some type of imagery. Some individuals can produce only thought images, those faint subjective representations which vary from the abstract to include memory and imagination of any sensory perception. Others can produce eidetic images, those which are very vivid, clear and colorful. This variation in ability suggests that when employing imagery, or visualizaion, the facilitator should encourage clients to use visual, auditory, or other sensory modalities for greater effectiveness.

Each individual may produce varying types of imagery during visualization techniques. Further, a person who is successful in evoking one type of imagery may not be successful in evoking another type. In general, factors to be aware of which influence imagery formation are:

1. innate ability to evoke imagery which has been nurtured through life experiences.
2. changes due to internal and environmental factors.
3. prior knowledge of what can be expected or the expectation the individual has about imagery.
4. the degree of awareness of emotional and mental states.
5. the degree of attention given to the technique; ie., from passive expectancy to extreme concentration.
6. the amount of regular practice intended to evoke imagery. [12]

Table 11 - 1

Types of Imagery

Thought and Memory Images

Thought Image: A faint, subjective representation, present in waking consciousness as part of an act or thought, which can be abstract or include memory and imagination of any sensory perception.

Eidetic Image: A projected image, generally visual but sometimes auditory, of such vividness, color, clarity, and differentiation of form as to seem to the fully awake subject like a percept; it may resemble greatly enhanced thought images or greatly prolonged afterimages.

Perceptual Images

Retinal Image: The image of external objects as focused on the retina of the eye.

Icon: A visual image, seen clearly so briefly, that it is perceived but not recognized or analyzed at the moment, but may nonetheless be further processed by the brain.

Entoptic Phenomena: Visual phenomena that have their stimulus in the eyeball; they occur after pressing the eyeball, a blow on the head, etc., and may appear as luminous dots, stars, swirls, or fire; they may also be hazy spots, specks, and hair-like objects that drift across the field of vision with movements of the eyes, as if hovering in space. These are due to floating impurities, such as red blood cells, that cast shadows on the retina. Further, phosphenes, which are subjective, luminous sensations, having more or less form, produced by pressure on the eyeball, the effort of accommodation, or an electric current. They appear as moving clouds of unsaturated color, relatively static network-like patterns, dots, or flashes.

Entotic Sounds: Sound sources which ordinarily pass unnoticed, but are registered in the brain in states of lowered as well as of heightened arousal. They are due to slight shifts in the states of contraction of the muscles of the middle ear.

Physiological Afterimage: Prolongation or renewal of a sensory experience after the external stimulus has ceased to operate. They are evoked by chemical changes and nerve reactions and may reproduce the qualities of the preceding perception as a positive, negative, or complementary after-image.

Illusion: A misinterpretation, taking the form of a sensation, which fails to represent the true character of a perceived object or objective situation.

Feeling State Imagery

Synesthesia: An actual perception of one type of sensation accompanied by the apparent sensation from another sensory modality, as in color hearing, in which sounds seem to have characteristic colors.

Body Image: The three-dimensional mental representation of the body in space, at rest or in motion, at any moment.

Dissociation: Feeling of separation from sensations, mental processes, the body image, or the environment.

Hallucinatory Images

Dream Image: Apparent sensory perceptions and motor activity, occurring in sleep, of such vividness as to appear real at the moment.

Hypnagogic Image: A suddenly appearing image, usually perceived as projected out in space, in the drowsy state just before sleep, of such vividness, clarity, and detail that it approaches sensory realism. It is usually visual, but can involve any other sense modality.

Hypnopompic Image: As the hypnagogic, but appearing after sleep in the half-waking state.

Hallucination: The experience of sensations or evocation of images with no real or external counterpart or cause. They may occure spontaneously or be induced or enhanced by certain physiological factors, chemicals, or other environmental conditions.

Adapted from Beata Jencks, *Your Body: Biofeedback at Its Best* (Chicago: Nelson Hall, 1977) pp. 28 & 29.

CONSCIOUS, INTENTIONAL IMAGERY

Conscious, intentional imagery means that the client freely employs the imagination in a controlled manner for a desired outcome. Jencks noted that "the proper use of the imagination requires that each individual choose and devise images which are most effective in achieving one's purpose."[13] Conscious, intentional imagery is contrasted with spontaneous imagery which is related to altered states of consciousness. Many forms of relaxation, as well as life experiences, create an altered state of consciousness. In this altered state, images or combinations of images may occur spontaneously. They may be sensations ranging from floating to vivid hallucinations. Facilitators should inform clients to expect spontaneous images which occur in the relaxed state. Further, it may be benefical to let clients decide whether a state of altered consciousness is to be induced purposefully or whether techniques should be deliberately kept short for use during daily relaxation practice.

When employing intentional, conscious imagery, the client, or client-therapist, should first use a sensing or thinking way to decide the desired outcome and then use the appropriate visualization technique to evoke sensations or reactions in a controlled way. When using past memories to evoke images, the memories should be of pleasant experiences. This enables clients to achieve the desired outcome without dredging up old negative emotions. This is particularly important when the facilitator is not trained to handle the disconcerting effects which may bubble-up from the subconscious.

With this background information, let us turn now to visualization techniques which can be utilized with clients in a general educational format to provide knowledge or skills for enhancing relaxation, self-involvement, security, or other pleasant sensations or actions. In short, the techniques can be used to assist clients' ability to cope with stress by inducing healthy psychophysiological reactions. They can be safely employed when clients are free to choose participation and the desired outcome. The facilitator should read and thoroughly understand all instructional pointers prior to implementation of specific techniques with clients. Even then, there is no guarantee a negative reaction will not occur.

The ideas and specific examples of visualization techniques are categorized according to intended outcomes: (1) enhance or deepen relaxation, (2) provide invigoration, (3) facilitate transitions, (4) positively affirm various aspects of self and enhance performance, and (5) reduce internal mental distractions. These are discussed separately but they may be combined to facilitate specific outcomes desired by clients.

IMAGERY FOR ENHANCEMENT OF RELAXATION

A number of techniques are available to enhance or deepen the relaxed state. Visualization of Relaxed Scenes is an excellent starting technique. The facilitator asks clients to recall from memory a happy, relaxed scene using the criteria that (1) it is free of negative memories and emotions, (2) it is a passive scene where there is little or no physical activity, and (3) it is so familiar that several of the senses can be employed. Relaxed scenes that meet these criteria might "include lying in the sun at the beach (maybe visualizing the waves as they roll into shore and then recede); relaxing in a small boat fishing on a comfortably warm day, the sun beating down and the body soaking up its warmth, and the boat lazily rocking in the water; relaxing in a cozy room in front of a fireplace and watching the flames flicker and dance; vacationing at a cottage on a trip."[14]

Visualization of a Relaxed Scene

   Imagine a pleasant scene, either something from your past, or a place where you might want to be in your imagination. It should be a situation in which you are merely pleasantly relaxed; not exhilarating and not boring, just very quiet, very pleasant, very relaxing. If you do not like this or cannot do it, just relax deeper and deeper with your exhalations. Exhale a few times gently, deeply, soothingly, calmly.[15]

• • • • • • • • INSTRUCTIONAL POINTERS • • • • • • • • •

1. *Allow clients to select their own relaxed scene. A person who almost drowned may not relax with a pleasant scene at the beach or floating lazily in a drifting boat. Someone who has experienced a fire may not relax watching the flames of a fireplace flicker and dance. Most of these negative situations can be eliminated by having clients choose their relaxed scene according to the criteria mentioned above.*

2. *The facilitator should allow clients to experience their scene using as many sense modalities as possible. When actually facilitating a relaxed scene, build the use of the senses into the phrasing. When clients are guiding themselves, give prior encouragement to use a variety of the senses to "feel, sense, and experience" the scene to its fullest.*

3. *If clients report only faint, subjective representations of a scene, let them know that the body is still responding to those images. To do this the facilitator can demonstrate the mind-body relationship with Cheveral's Pendulum, with a portable EMG biofeedback unit, or with temperature-sensitive liquid-crystal biofeedback cards.*

4. *Use of the imagination and breathing rhythm can lead to diverse visualization techniques. Encourage clients to vary techniques or adapt them, test them for effectiveness, based on individual needs.*

Imagined Breathing Pathways

Jencks combined imagery with the breathing rhythm for diverse purposes.[16,17] In these techniques imagery is employed to direct attention away from one or more of the usual breathing movements or pathways (Figure 11-1). Clients report that both the real and the imagined breathing pathways will lengthen and deepen respiration and ease tension, both of which are important in facilitating relaxation. Advanced techniques to ease pain can be developed from the basic technique presented here.

Figure 11 - 1

Real and Imagined
Breathing Pathways

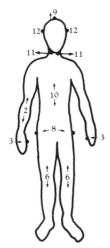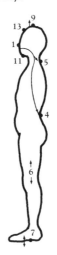

Breathing Pathway	Possible Outcomes
1. Through nose, mouth and throat	1. Release of tension, lengthen and deepen respiration of relaxation
2. Through the arms	2. Lengthen and deepen respiration
3. Through the hand	3. Collect and release tension in arms, shoulders
4. Through the small of the lower back	4. Allows respiration to ease & deepen; release muscular tension in lower back area
5. Through the back of the lower neck	5. Release of muscular tension in this area
6. Through the legs	6. Lengthen and deepen respiration
7. Through the bottom of foot	7. Collection and release of body tension
8. Through the hips	8. Diverts attention from normal breathing pathway
9. Through the crown of the head	9. May relieve tension headaches
10. Through a tube up and down torso	10. Relieves muscular tension and lengthens respiration
11. Through two holes under the chin, to the right and left of throat	11. May open congested sinuses
12. Through the temples	12. May relieve tension headaches
13. Through the forehead	13. May relieve tension headaches

Adapted from Beata Jencks, *Your Body: Biofeedback at Its Best* (Chicago: Nelson Hall, 1977), p. 134.

LONG BREATH

Assume a comfortable position, exhale, relax, and sink down into the supporting environment.

Exhale, relax, and allow your legs (upper legs, lower legs, ankles, feet) to become heavy as they are supported by the environment.

On the next exhalation, relax and let the entire trunk, hips, and buttocks sink into the environment. On the next breath, as you exhale, relax the upper arms, forearms, and hands. Exhale, relax, and allow the entire body to be supported by the surrounding environment.

Now, inhale through the nose. As you exhale, imagine, in a manner in which you are comfortable, the exhaled air flowing out through the bottom of the feet. Following each inhalation, visualize or think about that air flowing down the trunk, the legs, and permit the air to flow out through the feet (either the bottoms of the feet or out the toes). Feel, sense, and experience any sensations.

Repeat the above sequence on each successive breathing cycle for several cycles.

After three or four breathing cycles, simultaneously stretch, flex, inhale deeply, and open your eyes.[18]

•••••••• INSTRUCTIONAL POINTERS ••••••••

1. *It is beneficial to use both real (breathing in through the nose) and imagined (breathing out through the bottom of the feet) pathways as an introductory technique. Clients tend to report experiencing or sensing sensations of coolness, warmth, or tingling in parts of the body. These sensations usually occur near the location of the exhalation. When debriefing in a group, this technique reduces skepticism regarding use of the imagination.*

2. *During the long breath technique, the facilitator might suggest that clients:*

    a.   on the inhalation, imagine the breath streaming through the body as a color, e.g., red or blue.

    b.   develop an image for stress or tension and breathe that image out the body at the site of the exhalation.

3. *Some clients may report that the pathway from the nose to the feet is too long or that the breath got stuck in a specific body area on the way down. To avoid forcing the breath, or significantly altering the breathing rhythm, have clients shorten the exhalation pathway to the knees, palms or other locations within the body. Clients may also spontaneously adjust the pathway in some other creative manner.*

4. *As clients have success with one real and one imagined pathway, encourage them to:*

    a.   reverse the pathways, breathing in through the imagined pathway and exhaling through the nose.

    b.   use imagined pathways for both inhalation and exhalation.

5.   *As clients gain success in this basic exercise, discuss the adaptation of this technique for use with muscle tension or pain.*[19] *Any body area can be used for the specific purposes noted in Figure 11-1.*

IMAGERY FOR INVIGORATION

Oftentimes stress arises from the boredom of activities that demand prolonged attention. When this occurs, there are creative visualization techniques available to shake the cobwebs from the mind and/or provide stimulation and invigoration. When using the imagination for invigoration, the focus is on the inhalation phase of the breathing cycle rather than the exhalation phase (see Chapter 8 for inhalation sensations). However, both the inhalation and exhalation phases may be incorporated into invigoration techniques. Each of the three techniques presented here can be performed in just a few minutes and may be repeated from time to time throughout the day as needed. Other invigoration techniques can be easily generated for specific situations, environments, or as individual creativity allows.

The Spring Swirl

When attention lapses during mental work, close your eyes and focus your attention on your inhalations. (Be sure to breathe normally throughout this technique.)

Feel the coolness and vitality of the air as it flows into and through your nasal passages.

Without changing your natural breathing rhythm, imagine on the inhalation cool, fresh, spring air gently swirling around the inside of your head sweeping away tiredness and the cobwebs of the mind.

Feel, sense, and enjoy the invigoration.

When ready, flex-stretch-inhale and open your eyes. End on a refreshing *inhalation*.

Return to your routine or activity. [20]

The Tornado

On the inhalation, imagine the breath to be a cool, white tornado that swirls through the head.

On the exhalation, imagine the swirl moving rapidly down through the body and exiting at an imagined opening.

Repeat several times.

End on a deep inhalation which brings tension and invigoration into the body.

Return to your activity.

The Cold Waist Shower

Imagine standing in a shower with cold water pelting on your waist (your navel region).

Imagine the chilling effect radiating out from the waist region to the surrounding internal organs, stimulating and energizing them.

End on an inhalation and return to the rest of your day.

•••••••• INSTRUCTIONAL POINTERS ••••••••

1. Keep these techniques fairly short. Clients may perform them with their eyes open.

2. Encourage clients to develop their own invigoration techniques and then share them with others in the group.

3. Remind clients that focusing on the inhalation does not mean to force or deliberately change the natural breathing rhythm. The mental image that is created will cause specific sensations or physiological actions to occur.

FACILITATING TRANSITIONS

Transitions are made many times during each day. Whether it be shifting from sleep to an awake state, changing tasks at the work site, going from the work site to leisurely pursuits, or any one of a number of transitions made each day, these transitions demand pieces of our conscious attention. It is not uncommon that when transitions are made, the mind spontaneously moves back to the previous event and prevents full attention to the task at hand. The business person who arrives home to spend time with the family but is still thinking about work is not fully able to devote quality time to them. The executive who divides her morning into two, one and one-half hour blocks to work on projects A and B discovers that, as she begins work on project B, she has thoughts about project A racing through her head which interfere with giving full attenton to project B. The following visualization techniques are examples of how to use imagery to facilitate transitions so that more conscious attention can be given to the present.

The Clothes Hanger

As you remove your work clothing, article by article, imagine that you are hanging up your problems with the clothes.

As you remove a shirt or blouse, say to yourself that this piece of clothing represents the problem of John Doe and that it will remain in the closet this evening. As you do this, visualize old John Doe being hung up on the hanger.

The pants or skirt can represent a different problem, or one article, such as a coat or sweater, may represent all the problems - all the stressors and thoughts from work.

When you begin this technique, you will find that thoughts of work continue to enter your mind regularly. Don't worry about this or become frustrated. Each time you catch yourself thinking about your job, say, "Return to the hanger where I have put you - I'll take you off when I'm ready." Visualize the problems being hung up again.

If you practice this exercise faithfully, within a week or so you will probably make it through an evening with few thoughts about your job. When this occurs, you have made strides in regaining control of your thought processes.[21]

The Box

As you arrive home, imagine that a box with a lid is next to the door.

Before entering, exhale, relax, and imagine all of your thoughts of work flowing from your mind into the box. Then imagine the lid shutting.

Now you know where the thoughts are.

Again, if thoughts about your job come into your mind regularly, as they probably will at first, exhale and send them back to the box and shut the lid. If they persist, imagine a lock on the box and lock in the thoughts.

Don't be frustrated if these thoughts persist. With practice, you will notice them diminishing. Eventually you will be able to spend evenings, weekends, and vacations without thoughts of work, if you so desire.

If you must regularly or occasionally bring work home, put it away during supper, while playing with the children, or when getting ready for sleep. When you are ready to work, imagine the box opening and the thoughts coming to you.

Remain in control - you are the master of your conscious thoughts.[22]

The Blackboard

When trying to sleep, to change work projects, or to move from one aspect of your day to another, and you find thought after thought racing through your mind from past mental stimulation, assume a relaxed position.

Take a deep breath and slowly exhale.

Visualize or think about all the thoughts you wish to be rid of as being on a blackboard.

On each exhalation, imagine yourself erasing one of those thoughts from the board.

Do not hurry or be concerned about which thoughts you are erasing. Simply allow your mind to passively become more and more blank, more and more quiet as your mental blackboard becomes blank.

As you find your thoughts becoming fewer and fewer, you can switch to a relaxation technique as a passive means of changing focus from your thoughts to internal sensory sensations.

When mental stimulation has been reduced, flex-stretch-inhale and open your eyes.

•••••••• INSTRUCTIONAL POINTERS ••••••••

1. *Discuss several of these ideas with your clients prior to having them try them on their own. It is important to reinforce the idea that clients should develop and implement techniques that are acceptable to them and meet a specific need. Encourage clients to adapt or develop their own techniques.*

2. *Encourage clients to share ways they have used imagery for specific purposes in the past or the successes or setbacks they have had in trying to use imagery techniques for making transitions.*

POSITIVE AFFIRMATIONS

Since birth each of us has been making affirmations of one sort or another. These affirmations have come through self-talk, attitudes, emotions and behaviors which blend together to create an evolving self-image. Life experiences have a way of muddying and eroding self-image thereby limiting the development of our innate potentials. Behaviors can be relearned with appropriate awareness, self-talk and attitudes. Thus, affirmations (also known as special formulas and self-suggestions) are a deliberate input of information with subsequent emotions and images which serve to change thought processes and behaviors.

Affirmations are short and positive statements to facilitate the achievement of specific goals. They are ways to change one's self-talk and to relabel perceptions of life events that foster a more positive self-concept. Affirmations work because of the body-mind relationship. The self-talk, thoughts and attitudes held about self and/or life events are translated into symbolic mental pictures. These pictures create emotions (feelings) which in turn are manifested as an action or behavior.

The focus of affirmations is not on the behavior but on the self-esteem of the person. Constructive visualization with positive statements is used to generate new emotional responses. The affirmations are catalysts for new self-talk, which can lead to the desired outcome. Since these affirmations are repeated consciously, they are held foremost in the subconscious mind allowing the individual to eventually respond as affirmed.

Affirmation statements can be used to move toward the accomplishment of *do* goals. *Do* goals are those goals that involve what you wish to accomplish personally, in your job, or at home. Personally it may be to lose weight or alleviate worry; professionally, it may be to give a great presentation at the next board meeting; for an athlete, it may be the pursuit of a personal best. Statements repeated in this context involve doing.

Additionally, there are *be* goals. *Be* goals may also be set for self, family, or work. These goals include the development of personal qualities as determined by personal values and standards. They center on the processes of becoming rather than doing. A father who wishes to become more loving, for example, may focus affirmations on extending love to family members.

Affirmations should be realistic, simple, acceptable and convincing to the person who uses them. These statements cannot fool the mind into believing the impossible. Perfection statements like "I always" or "everytime" are irrational and should be avoided. One should only affirm as high as one can honestly imagine becoming or performing.

Other guidelines for developing affirmations include:

1. Affirm only self. The focus of affirmations is on personal qualities or situations. It is a deliberate attempt to control information and visualization that brings about changes in thoughts, attitudes or opinions.

2. All statements should be positive. Statements should focus on what you will *do* or *become*, not on what you will not do or on what you are trying to avoid. Statements should portray the image of "I am relaxed," rather than "I am not tense," to the subconscious.

3. Use the present tense. Change comes from sensing, feeling and experiencing the desired change *now*. It is important that these statements and images be translated to the subconscious as if one's eyes are actually viewing the achieved goals and the subsequent emotional and behavorial responses. The more a person subsconsciously acts as if he/she already possesses the desired outcome, the more noticeable will be the change in self-image and/or behavior.

4. Use action words. Words used in affirming statements generate images and emotions. Action words like energetic, enthusiastic, and happy create more vivid emotions and pictures of the desired outcome - all while in a relaxed and anxious-free state.

5. Avoid comparisons. Affirmations are a personal matter. One is striving to achieve or develop personal potentials. Comparison statements like "better than" or "as good as" undermine achieving one's own very best. Avoid these phrases when evaluating progress. The goal is to be more satisfied with oneself rather than to compare oneself with others.

The following affirmations are listed according to specific intended outcomes. These are just a few examples of the many possible affirmations and outcomes.

To build confidence:
> I am peforming to my ability.
> I succeed because I believe I can.

To improve concentration:
> I am absorbed in. . .
> I am focused completely on (the task).

To promote a positive mental attitude:
> I am happy and content.
> I am healthy, happy and strong.

To foster relaxation:
> I am calm and relaxed.
> I am letting go of unnecessary tension.

To foster health and healing:
> I am healthy, refreshed, and energized.
> I am pain free, happy me.

To prepare for sport competition:
> I am ready.
> I am giving my best.

To foster self-image:
> I like and respect myself.
> I am capable of expressing myself and
> I allow others to express themselves.

106

•••••••• INSTRUCTIONAL POINTERS ••••••••

1. *Affirmations are most effective when combined with mental images of the desired outcome. Keeping a mental picture on one's mental screen while repeating the affirmation allows one to use more than one sense modality in the experience.*

2. *As with other techniques, clients should repeat the affirmation in time with the exhalation, stop for the inhalation, and repeat it again on the exhalation.*

3. *Although affirmations can be repeated and visualized in an unrelaxed state, a relaxed state allows clients to visualize and affirm free of anxiety. This guides clients into a state of relaxation using the technique which works best.*

REDUCTION OF INTERNAL DISTRACTIONS

Constant and unrelenting stimuli from the external environment can create an unrelenting internal chattering of the mind. This internal dialogue can be more difficult to overcome than reducing environmental stimuli. Techniques for reducing internal distractions are similar to techniques for facilitating transitions mentioned earlier in this chapter. The primary difference is that the reduction of internal mental stimuli is sought for its own sake and not for the intended outcome of making a transition. Each of the following examples of how to reduce internal chatter uses both the exhalation phase of the breathing cycle and imagery. Each approach can be employed for as long or short a time as clients desire.

1. As you become aware of distractions, inhale, say "stop," exhale and allow the thought to slowly dissolve from your mind. Repeat the exhalation for several more breaths until the mind becomes more and more blank.
2. Imagine windshield wipers swishing back and forth on your mental screen clearing away your mental distractions. Allow the wipers to slow with your exhalations as your chatter slows.
3. Imagine a white, puffy cloud descending toward you. As the cloud engulfs your head, you see the distractions placed upon it. Then, with succeeding exhalations, gently blow the cloud away with all your distractions.

• • • • • • • • • INSTRUCTIONAL POINTERS • • • • • • • •

1. *Since the purpose of these suggestions is to reduce the internal chattering of the mind, suggest that clients use only one of these at a time. If after several times the suggestion is ineffective, encourage the client to select another idea.*

2. *These suggestions include the use of imagery; some include the use of a word or statement. Thus, the facilitator can flexibly incorporate these ideas where appropriate. They may be used as a separate category for relaxation or be included as part of previously mentioned techniques.*

CHAPTER 12

MEDITATION

The word meditation conjures up visions of strangely garbed gurus, Eastern mystical rites, and initiates lost in another world as they seek their inner self through altered states of consciousness. It is unfortunate that the process of meditation has developed such connotations because the meditative process is actually much more simple than most people realize—yet more profound. Let us explore the meditative process and attempt to understand what it is at a basic level.

WHAT IS MEDITATION?

Meditation is a technique and process of training one's mind to be attentive. Rather than allowing one's mind to wander from thought to thought, perception to perception, or feeling to feeling without any control, the meditative process helps train the mind to focus on what the individual chooses. Through this process, over an extended period of time, the inner workings of one's mind become less hectic and more stable.

Descriptions of the meditation process include the following:

At this most universal level, all meditation systems are variations on a single process for transforming consciousness... The strongest agreement among meditation schools is on the importance of retraining attention.[1]

. . . it is important to define meditation and dispel the misconception that meditation is contemplation, rumination, or thinking about a concept. Meditation is an experiential exercise involving an individual's actual attention, not belief systems or other cognitive processes . . . the fundamental process of meditation is to gain mastery over attention.[2]

It [meditation] includes two processes: making the mind concentrated or one-pointed, and bringing to total cessation the turning of the mind.[3]

Meditation involves any activity which attempts to focus and maintain attention on a single, repetitive, or unchanging stimulus.[4]

Meditation refers to a family of techniques which have in common a conscious attempt to focus attention in a non-analytical way, and an attempt not to dwell on discursive, ruminating thought.[5]

This last definition provides the most clearly understandable explanation. Meditation should not be seen merely as a process of staring at a candle flame in an incense-filled room while sitting cross-legged on a Japanese pillow. Remove all of the trappings associated with individual idiosyncrasies of meditators and one can discover that the actual meditative process is in the mind's gentle struggle for attentiveness: in this instance the simple perception of the candle flame.

While it is simple to observe such perceptions, it is difficult to maintain a directed attentiveness to the candle flame while the mind strays from the task and fills with thoughts, subjective feelings, and the like. Anyone can see a candle flame, but how many can continue to merely see the candle flame without mental talk about its color or shape, memories about other experiences with candles, emotive feelings associated with such memories, and so on?

Our minds continue an internal dialogue almost every waking moment of our lives. And, if you include dream time while asleep, the mind spends almost all of its time in mental activity. Actually, such a continual flow of thoughts is important in our daily process of living. Without the rapid, analytical process of perception, the integration of perception with memory, and the consequent interaction with our environment, it would be impossible to perform simple tasks like crossing a busy street or ordering a meal from a restaurant menu. In fact, the rapid generation and continual processing of ideas provides man with the creative material that has made him the master of his environment. Through his capacity to formulate mental pictures of the future as it could be, and his analytical process to determine the feasibility of such dreams, man can mold the future.

However, the mind of man can be an enemy at times. Although ruminations of the mind can create insight and innovation, the mind can also generate excessive worries or pessimistic perspectives of reality. Fears of failure or rejection can be blown out of proportion, resulting in anxiety-related physiological reactions, even though the subjective threat is not necessarily existent or valid. Unfortunately, the body reacts to mentally constructed threats as if they were true, allowing stress reactions to build up in the body's systems. Psychological reactions can compound upon other psychological reactions in a vicious cycle, feeding upon themselves, until the person becomes physically or mentally ill.

The practice of meditation does not propose that individuals learn to quiet all of the internal dialogue of the mind. Instead, the practice of meditation suggests quieting the mind, through attentiveness training, for brief periods of time. That balance of activity and stillness of mental processes provides a more harmonious condition overall, enhancing the mental processes during everyday, active life.

WHAT MEDITATION IS NOT

A discussion of what meditation is not can further help to clarify the process of meditation.

MEDITATION IS NOT RELIGIOUS IN NATURE

First and foremost, it is important to realize that meditation is not bound to any religious doctrine. The fact that meditation is used in both Eastern and Western religions does not mean that meditation is religious in context. Meditation has been used as a tool in Eastern and Western religions to help novitiates gain further understanding into themselves and their religion, but that does not make the practice of meditation religious in nature. For the same reason that wearing robes does not make a monk religious, the practice of meditation does not mean you are professing any religion. It is also important to note that, historically, the process of meditation has had as important a background in Western Judaeo-Christian religions as it has had in the Eastern religions of Buddhism, Taoism, Hinduism, and others. The Middle Ages, a time of great strength for the Christian church, is filled with examples of cloistered monks and nuns having revelatory experiences as they meditate on their Creator. Even today the churches are explaining many old and new ways to pray, which include the meditative process as one example.[6]

MEDITATION IS NOT CONTEMPLATION

When one contemplates upon an idea, activity, or object, the mind is engaged in remembering and generating associations for analysis. To contemplate on an apple, the mind becomes filled with associations: apple trees, seeds to plant, fresh squeezed cider, the beauty of a red Delicious apple, an apple a day keeps the doctor away, the importance of fruit in one's diet, and more. But to meditate on an apple is to merely observe the apple as if it were the first apple you had ever observed - to quiet the mind of all associative thoughts so that analysis does not take precedence over attentive observation. How difficult this is! And how rarely we actually participate in such fresh observation. Thus, meditation can be considered almost the opposite of contemplation. Meditation is a quieting of the analytic mind, while contemplation is allowing the free-associating mind to run on. We contemplate much more frequently than we meditate. An Eastern sage might say to one of his disciples: "Don't think of a monkey!" to observe how much control the disciple has over his ruminating mind. Can the disciple calm his mind enough to follow the sage's suggestion? Or does the sage's suggestion send the disciple's mind into a flurry of questions and thoughts about monkeys, what the sage meant, or the philosophical implications of the statement?

MEDITATION IS NOT A LOSS OF MENTAL CONTROL

While meditating, the meditator does not lose control of his or her mind to any greater being or to another individual. Meditators stay mentally alert and in possession of their physical faculties at all times. Although there may be alterations in the individual's state of consciousness as the individual meditates, the meditator has no difficulty ending the meditation whenever he or she chooses to do so. Any loss of control attributed to meditation is probably due to the subject falling into a dreamy reverie (hypnagogic state) or into a sleep state.

MEDITATION IS NOT SLEEP

While meditation is occurring, the mind is alert, yet passive. The process of meditation requires the individual to maintain control of the situation by not allowing the mind to slow down and reach a drowsy state that induces sleep. In fact, the temptation to sleep while meditating is considered by many meditating groups to be one of the more difficult traps that inexperienced meditators must learn to cope with. Falling asleep actually demonstrates to the meditator that control of the mind is still eluding him, or that he has accumulated too much sleep deprivation to allow the meditative process to occur.

In actuality, meditation and other relaxation techniques are considered more restful than sleep. Although the mind may still be at a self-conscious state, the stillness of the mind brings about a myriad of physiological changes that allow the body to reach a deeply relaxed state. Sleep may or may not be restful, depending upon the sleeping environment, the level of agitation of the mind as it dreams, and other factors.

MEDITATION IS NOT A PANACEA

Although the physiological and psychological benefits of meditation have been documented,[7] it is important to comment that meditation is not the long sought for solution to everyone's problems: it is not *the* answer to the ills of mankind. Meditation does have beneficial effects on both experienced and beginning meditators, and many individuals consider it the one technique that works best for them, but meditation is not for everyone. The process of meditation has a variety of forms to fit with a variety of meditator personalities, but many beginning meditators still find that they are not satisfied with their initial results and turn to other activities for self-growth or relaxation.

This last point needs further expansion. Meditation is often touted as a method to reach sudden, mystical insights into the workings of the world or the individual, and that all one has to do to obtain such revelations is to sit back a few minutes and wait for it to happen. Not true! The choice to practice meditation may be a quick decision, but the impact of meditation on the practitioner is subtle and gradual. Yes, some meditators reach enlightening perspectives on themselves or the world in a flash of insight, but it usually takes many months of regular, dedicated meditation sessions as a preparation for such experiences. Meditation generates more subtle ways of reacting with the environment, people, and the meditator that aid in stress management, so don't look for today's improvement over yesterday's condition. Most experienced meditators will comment that the effects of meditation are gradual, and that the actual expectation for improvements is a trap into which many beginners fall.

MEDITATION IS NOT JUST A RELAXATION TECHNIQUE

Meditation, as a process, has been performed for a variety of purposes ranging from developing a greater clarity of mental thought to enhancing religious experiences to aiding phobics in the clinical psychologist's office. The use of meditative techniques as a relaxation technique is just one of the variety of reasons why meditation is practiced in the Western and Eastern worlds. To relegate meditation as just another relaxation technique is to ignore its history and its many roles in past and current civilizations. As mentioned earlier, meditation was used as a mental training device in many settings, especially within the Western and Eastern religious training centers. For the purpose of this textbook, however, meditation is presented as a relaxation strategy for enhancing psychological and physiological well being.

MEDITATION PRELIMINARIES

There are three major guidelines that encompass the process of beginning meditation. These are: correct environment, correct body, and correct mind. We will look at these one at a time and explore the various points that lead to good meditation experiences.

CORRECT ENVIRONMENT

The individual who desires to meditate is naturally surrounded by an environment. Any environmental factors which detract from the mind's ability to focus attention make the meditative process more difficult to the beginner. Thus, proper selection of an environment for meditation practice is important. The points in this section are very similar to the major points considered in Chapter 1, The Environment for Relaxation Training. This discussion will reinforce these points, and provide environmental control suggestions that are particularly relevant to meditators.

Choose a room or space which is as free of distractions as possible. Visit the site at the same time of the day on the same day of the week for your meditation practices. Factors such as room temperature, the presence of a telephone that might ring, overly bright or dim lights, or even excessive room draftiness can hamper the beginner's practice. Although meditation is not expected to be performed in a perfectly quiet and still environment, the closer the site is to this optimum the less difficult initial practice will be. Later on, when the meditator is more experienced, other environments with more distractive elements can be adequate. After all, meditation is not meant to be performed in ideal environments only - it's just easier on beginners to start that way.

Choose an environment that is psychologically neutral as well as physically comfortable. If the chosen site easily brings back distressing memories or happy experiences, the practice of meditation may be distracted frequently. Meditating out of doors on a pleasant sunny day may be possible for some, but the vibrant songs of birds, the busy hum and honking of nearby traffic, and the wind whistling through nearby trees may make the practice more difficult than easy.

Encourage clients to take initiative and claim a meditation space as their own for the brief time they spend there. A carefully chosen space can control interruptions beneficially. For example, if a client chooses a room at home to practice in, other family members should know that this time and place is off limits so that the client can be alone. A sign proclaiming: "PLEASE DO NOT DISTURB!" or "MEDITATION IN PROCESS. LET ME HAVE PEACE AND QUIET." can help insure such quiet time for a client. If, for example, clients wish to meditate in a work environment, they should pick a time that almost guarantees no distractions: the few minutes before everyone else arrives for work, the lunchtime slow period, the few minutes during afternoon break, or the few minutes just after everyone else has left for the day. They should also disconnect the phone for these few minutes of quiet time and let the office mates know they plan to take a few minutes of quiet time. the client does not have to say, "I'm meditating," if there are fears that others will find some uncomfortable ways to joke about it. Instead, the client can just let them know, "I'm aware of the impact that stress can have on my job quality, my home life, and my health. One way I cope is to take ten to fifteen minutes of quiet time to relax and recharge." This way, the client will gain their support, if not their respect.

CORRECT BODY

Once the environment is carefully chosen to begin the process of meditation, it is important to prepare the body. Your client doesn't necessarily have to "cleanse the body of all impurities" before beginning meditation. But a few common sense ideas should be kept in mind during preparation. All of these ideas stem from the basic tenet of reducing distractions that allow the client's mind to wander from the object of attention. Have the client heed his or her body messages before beginning practice.

Correct posture is invaluable to meditation. The body sends a multitude of messages to the brain if the body is uncomfortable or under physical stress. With correct posture, muscles can relax as much as is possible and allow the meditative practice to continue with a minimum of commentary from the body's physiological systems. With the back straight, the head balanced correctly over the cervical vertebrae, and the hips flexed forward slightly, the body is balanced with minimal muscle tension. Correct postures include, but are not necessarily limited to, Yogic asanas (postures) that are frequently associated with meditation. Sitting on a raised pillow with both feet folded in front of the body may look strange, but this and other postures have been shown scientifically to minimize muscular strain while aiding correct posture of the body. This does not mean, however, that everyone must now meditate in an unfamiliar posture! Sitting upright in a comfortable chair with sound back, arm, and neck support can do just as well for beginning meditators. Again, the key to choosing a posture is to find one that minimizes bodily distractions for the mind during the meditative process. Please examine the basic positions described in Chapter 6, Basic Relaxation Positions, to find a posture that best matches the client's body physiology. The client should be able to tell you after a little experimentation what basic posture feels most comfortable.

The one exception to this general rule about posture is the sleeping position. Too many beginners start their meditation session lying on a bed and wind up taking a nap. As one might expect, the body and mind perceive this horizontal posture as a cue to begin the sleep process. By sitting upright in a comfortable posture, the body can maintain a relaxed state, yet not get so comfortable as to drop off to sleep.

An overtired body can hamper meditation practice. Instead of reaching an alert yet passive state of mind, the mind can drop into a dreamy reverie and then into sleep. Since meditation practice does quiet the body and mind, beginners who have not maintained appropriate sleeping habits will have difficulty staying awake. In a sense, the body seizes the opportunity to grab a few winks to make up for lost sleep. The remedy is quite simple: help the client evaluate his or her sleep habits to see if more rest is needed. It can become a problem for meditation practice if your client uses meditation time to catnap. A client who regularly drifts off to sleep instead of meditating will find it more difficult to stay alert in future practice sessions for meditation. For this reason clients should not try to meditate just before going to sleep. Lying in bed just before bedtime will give the client more time sleeping, not meditating.

Meditation time and meal time do not mix well. If the mind is constantly interrupted by thoughts of hunger and delicious foods or by rumblings of an empty, eager stomach anticipating food, meditation time will be jeopardized. Such distractions make it difficult to focus the mind. Conversely, a stomach that has just been filled with a most delicious meal may also lead to difficulties during meditation. The body responds to the ingestion of a meal by secreting more acid into the stomach, releasing alkaline factors into the blood, and increasing stimulation to the parasympathetic nervous system (the rest-and-repose autonomic nervous system). These bodily activities make it easier for an individual to fall asleep, as anyone who has laid down after a big Sunday dinner can attest. Meditation time can sometimes work well after a light meal, but should be moved away from larger meal times if at all possible.

Help clients learn to create a comfortable body condition prior to meditation. They can perform a brief scan of body areas for itches, cold spots, pressure sites, and other complaints that could distract the meditation practice. Help clients remedy these body distractions as much as you can. They can scratch that itch, kick off those tight shoes, or undo their tight belt. In essence, help clients plan ahead so that the mind doesn't begin to use the body as an excuse to not attend to the meditation.

One final thought about correct body: clients should not feel that they must play the martyr as they go through a meditation. In other words, if they develop an itch, they should scratch it. If their buttocks get too sore to ignore, have them slowly shift their position until their buttocks are comfortable and meditation is again possible. They should not ignore, with gritted teeth, the fly that is determined to land on every square inch of their head and face; they should get up and swat the fly or move the meditation practice to a new room. After all, ten to fifteen minutes of continually interrupted meditation is not truly meditating. The struggle is to train the mind to be attentive.

CORRECT MIND

The correct mind for meditation is the most difficult to explain. Meditation is in some ways ineffable - one needs to experience it before one can truly understand what it is like. But let us examine some major points.

At times the mind may be likened to a young child. A young child likes to do what it wants to do and finds it difficult to sit still for brief periods of time. Such a child may find it difficult to learn self-discipline or how to postpone self-gratification. In many ways the mind is like this, too. When trying to focus the mind on one object of attention, the mind may wander away to more exciting, varied stimulation. When helping a child learn how to perform a particular task, an adult trainer would try to be patient and supportive throughout the process. Instead of negative criticisms for every time that the child wanders away from the task, the adult trainer would gently remind the child what task needs performing and would say to himself or herself, "I must be patient with this child. Immaturity and a short attention span are characteristics of youth. I must be gentle in guiding the child back onto the task at hand so that I do not make the task become burdensome or disliked." In the same way, the meditator must be gentle and forgiving with the mind. Mental distractions will come into the meditation process. They should not be seen as symptoms of failure because they occur in the meditations of beginning and advanced meditators alike. Perhaps the best approach to the ruminations that interfere with a meditative technique is to merely laugh at how untrained the mind is, gently empty the mind of the distraction, and get on with the meditation practice. There is no need to curse, become disappointed, or mentally kick oneself. It is best to get back to the meditation technique with a minimal amount of further distraction. This gentle but directed mental activity during meditation has been called "passive volition" or "mental passivity," but it is not a completely passive condition. The mind is focused, but does not force any thoughts in or out.

One must be cautioned, however, that there is the other side of the coin to this problem. Taking a laissez-faire attitude towards meditation, especially in the regular practice of a meditative technique, can lead to meditation becoming " one more technique in the multitude of techniques that just don't work for me." Meditation demands a certain amount of commitment and regularity for it to work, and that commitment requires a serious attitude on the part of the beginning meditator. It is very easy for beginning meditators to practice for ten or eleven days, not see any differences, and then decide that meditation doesn't work for them. It is more difficult for a beginning meditator to practice regularly, giving it an honest try for about one month, and then make a decision as to whether meditation has had any impact.

Depending upon the type and focus of a meditative technique, the beginning meditator should be careful of what is called "The Law of the Good Moment".[8] This law exemplifies how beginning meditators can get emotionally (and egotistically) caught up in their own meditation results. If, for example, the beginning meditator focuses on the inhalation and exhalation of the breath and mentally remarks, "Wow! Look at me! I'm really meditating!" the beginning meditator is no longer meditating. The mental process of the mind observing itself trying to meditate, and then commenting to itself that the beginning meditator has achieved the meditative state, is actually another distraction that has taken the mind away from true meditation. If a person thinks while meditating that he or she is doing a great job, that person is not! Evaluating the meditative experience after the meditation is over is acceptable, but introducing evaluative thoughts during the meditation should be avoided.

•••••••• INSTRUCTIONAL POINTERS ••••••••

1. *The meditative process should not be attempted if the individual feels unduly uncomfortable with the idea of meditating. This also means that a meditation technique should not be continued if the client feels uncomfortable with the technique during the actual meditation.*

2. *Some individuals object to the concept of meditation and may have firmly held beliefs or connotations that will not yield to any educational efforts on the part of the facilitator. In other individuals, educational efforts may allay any fears they have about meditation. In general, it is wise to explore with clients their beliefs about and reactions to the idea of meditating before the meditation training process begins. For some clients, calling meditation an "attentiveness training exercise" or a "mental relaxation technique" may be sufficient to divorce all the negative and positive connotations from the practice of meditation.*

3. *In actuality, many relaxation tactics currently being taught are thinly disguised meditations that have the mind enter a deeply relaxed state through the process of gently focusing the mind upon an object, thought, sound, or sensation. Whether the meditation techniques are called a meditation or are called something else, the clients should understand that they can stop the meditation process if it becomes uncomfortable.*

4. *However, be careful that this is not used as an excuse by the meditator's undisciplined mind to avoid the meditative process altogether. Since there is some mental discipline involved during meditation, the mind may try to talk itself out of the continuation of the experience. Clients can often tell the difference between a recalcitrant mind and a truly uncomfortable gut feeling about the meditative process; this should be their guide.*

ONE MEDITATION TECHNIQUE

This monologue could be used to guide clients in a basic concentrative breath meditation. It is not meant to be the only way to teach a concentrative breath meditation, nor is it meant to be the only major type of meditation to teach. There are hundreds of meditations that could be taught, some easier and some harder than this one. Obviously, this chapter can only begin to scratch the surface of meditation instruction, a topic on which many ancient and modern books have been written. The monologue points the way for doing a basic meditation, and integrates the many points discussed so far in this chapter.

Allow yourself to get comfortable in your chair. If it will help you relax more, take off your shoes or loosen your belt a bit.

Settle in and, when you are ready, comfortably scan your body for any cold spots, itchy areas, or tight clothing. Go ahead and cover up those cold spots or scratch the itches you feel. Allow yourself to get as comfortable as possible.

Check your basic body posture, and gently move about until your back is fully supported. You can also slowly rotate your head until it feels comfortably balanced on your neck. If you notice any muscle tension in your body, gently reposition yourself so that the tension is gone. Gently scan for tension, and relax...your ankles...legs...hips...back...chest...arms...neck...head... and face...

When you are ready, allow your eyes to close, and gradually turn your attention to your breathing. Do not try to alter your breathing. Just simply watch your breathing as you inhale...and exhale...inhale...and exhale....

As we begin this meditation, remember that you are in control. Your mind is alert but calm...and still.... Feel free to reach down and scratch any itch or handle any distraction, but remember to gently turn your mind back to your meditation. Allow yourself to comfortably relax during the meditation.

As you exhale this next time, gently count to yourself: ONE.... As you exhale your next breath, gently count to yourself: TWO.... As you exhale your third breath, gently count: THREE.... As you exhale your fourth breath, gently count: FOUR.... And as you exhale the fifth breath, count to yourself: FIVE.... For your next breath, begin counting at ONE again, so that you gently count your exhalations to yourself in cycles of five. Gently count your exhalations for a few cycles....

If any thoughts, feelings or sensations distract you from your meditation on your breaths, gently push them out of your mind. Then go back to gently counting your exhalations.... If you find you can't remember the next number or you have counted higher than five, don't worry. That's O.K. Just begin counting at number one again....

Continue to count your exhalations in cycles of five. Feel comfortable that there is no place you need to be right now except here...that there is nothing else you have to do right now except what you are doing.... Continue the meditation, counting your exhalations....

(after ten to fifteen minutes of meditation)

There is no rush to do anything. Allow yourself to be where you are: relaxed, comfortable and still. When you feel you are ready, gradually allow your mind and your body to become a little more alert and a little more active.

Focus your attention on your inhalations, and permit your inhalations to grow during the next few breathing cycles.... On your next inhalation, take in a deep breath, stretch your arms over your head, and let your body become more alert and more active as your mind and body comes back to a normal level of energy. Welcome back!

A MEDITATION REGIMEN

One of the common questions beginning meditators ask is: "How often and how long should I meditate?" There is no one correct answer to this question, but many meditation instructors suggest that a beginner practice meditation once or, at most, twice a day. For a beginning meditator, ten to twenty minutes per meditation session is sufficient to help the meditator discover whether meditation is a beneficial practice to him or her and to determine how to fit the practice of meditation into a busy time schedule. As the subject moves into the intermediate stages of meditation training, each meditation session can grow in length, and other types of meditations can be practiced on a regular basis.

CHAPTER 13

BIOFEEDBACK:
AN INTRODUCTION

During the past ten years, biofeedback has become an integral part of stress management programs. Practitioners are becoming aware that biofeedback training holds great potential not only for the alleviation of specific stress-related symptoms but also for facilitating the development of physiological awareness necessary for learning stress-management skills. This chapter discusses the theory and practice of biofeedback in stress-management, including guidelines for facilitators who wish to incorporate biofeedback into their stress-management programs.

WHAT IS BIOFEEDBACK?

Biofeedback can be defined as the use of sensitive instruments to detect physiological changes in the body, convert these changes into observable signals, and relay this information back to the client. An important outcome of this process is that the individual can learn to exert *control* over the physiological changes being monitored. Some of the physiological changes include changes in muscle tension, blood flow, skin electrical conductance, and brain wave activity. Clinical and educational uses of biofeedback assume that learned control over these functions will reduce stress-related symptoms. An extensive body of literature demonstrates how biofeedback achieves this goal.[1]

CLINICAL VS. EDUCATIONAL APPLICATIONS

Broadly speaking, there are two areas of application of biofeed-back, clinical and educational. Clinical biofeedback applies biofeed-back to treat a physical or psychological symptom, usually stress-related, for which an individual might ordinarily seek medical or psychological treatment. *Educational* applications, on the other hand, use biofeedback to gain increased awareness of physiological changes in the body in order to improve one's ability to manage stress, seek deeper self-understanding, and gain a clearer appreciation of the mind-body connection. There is a good degree of overlap between these two fields of application; however, if clear physical symptoms of stress are apparent, the individual should seek a medical evaluation prior to seeking biofeedback treatment. Table 13-1 illustrates some of the physiological and psychological symptoms for which biofeedback, as part of a treatment approach, has demonstrated some degree of success. These symptoms are stress-related in that stress has been shown either to play a significant role in the origin of the disease (such as cardiovascular dysfunction) or to exert a significant influence over the course of the disease (such as diabetes). The following section presents a brief overview of how biofeedback is used clinically in the treatment of several common stress-related symptoms.

Table 13 - 1

Disorders and Conditions for which Biofeedback has been used as a Treatment Modality

anxiety disorders
asthma
blepharospasm
bruxism
cardiac arrhythmias
causalgia
cerebral palsy
costochondritis
dermatitis
diabetes
dysmenorrhea and other
    menstrual distress
educational applications
enuresis nocturna
epilepsy
esophageal motility disorders/
    dysphagia
fecal incontinence
hemifacial spasm
hemiplegia or hemiparesis
    due to stroke
hyperhidrosis
hyperkinesia
hypertension, essential
hypertonic/spastic muscles
inflammatory bowel disease
    (ulcerative colitis, Crohn's)

insomnia
irritable bowel syndrome
learning disabilities
myofacial pain disorders
neuromuscular disorders, orthopedics
pain, chronic
Parkinson's disease
paretic muscles
personal growth
preventive medicine/health maintenance
Raynaud's disease/syndrome
sexual disorders
spinal cord injuries
    (incomplete lesions)
stuttering
tendon transfer
tension headaches (i.e., muscle
    contraction)
tic
tinnitus
torticollis
unrinary incontinence/retention
vascular headaches
vasoconstrictive disorders
writer's cramp

CLINICAL BIOFEEDBACK APPLICATIONS

Muscle Contraction Headache

One of the most common stress-related symptoms for which biofeedback has demonstrated clinical utility is muscle-contraction (tension) headache. It has been estimated that approximately 90% of all headaches are tension related. It is thought that the dull, aching, band-like pain results from sustained contractions of the head, neck, and jaw muscles over time. The electromyograph (EMG) biofeedback instrument provides immediate feedback of muscle tension levels, enabling the client to develop increased control over these varying tension levels. Most clinicians believe that it is not enough for the client to practice EMG biofeedback training once or twice a week in a clinic. They believe it must be combined with regular relaxation exercises outside the clinic in order to learn the control necessary to alleviate the tension-related pain. The Biofeedback Society of America, in one of its task force reports, concluded that EMG biofeedback relaxation training combined with home practice of relaxation will alleviate or eliminate muscle-contraction headaches in 70% or more of the cases.[2]

Migraine Headaches

Another common type of headache pain is the vascular or migraine headache. Most researchers believe that migraine symptoms stem from excessive constriction of the arteries supplying the scalp and brain followed by excessive dilation of these arteries. The resulting crucial pain symptoms often cannot be alleviated by medication. The excessive constriction of the arteries supplying the scalp usually occurs as part of a generalized stress reaction and is often accompanied by a decrease in blood flow to the hands, resulting in the familiar symptom of cold hands. Consequently, thermal biofeedback training, with the goal of warming the hands, is effective in helping migraine clients prevent the occurrence of migraine symptoms provided the handwarming process occurs *before* the actual onset of headache pain.

The usual training strategy for teaching skin temperature control uses thermal sensors to detect and display changing finger temperature, so that clients learn to warm the fingers voluntarily. Once again, to be effective, this training must be combined with regular home practice in finger warming. For example, a migraine sufferer might spend five minutes practicing finger warming in the morning before arising, and repeatedly throughout the day, in order to prevent the onset of migraine symptoms. Not all sufferers of migraine headache, however, are able to significantly alleviate their pain symptoms. Many other factors likely contribute to the occurrence of migraine symptoms, ranging from environmental and dietary influences to the effects of secondary gain; that is, many clients are unwilling to give up their migraine symptoms in part because these periodic symptoms afford them secondary rewards (e.g., freedom from excessive responsibility, attention from significant others) which they do not know how to obtain by more direct methods. Nonetheless, thermal biofeedback assisted relaxation strategies provide hope for many migraine sufferers who wish to reduce both the frequency and severity of their symptoms.

Raynaud's Syndrome and Phenomenon

Raynaud's syndrome is a potentially severe disorder of the peripheral circulatory system resulting from excessive constriction of blood vessels in the hands and feet. Exposure to cold stimulation or emotional stress may trigger attacks. In more severe cases, excessive and sustained constriction of the blood flow causes severe pain with possible onset of gangrene if the vasospasm is not reversed. Surgical treatments via sympathectomy have yielded unreliable results, and medication intended to reduce that vasospasm, while providing some symptomatic relief, may cause intolerable side effects. When using thermal biofeedback training to relieve vasospasms, clients report up to a fifty percent reduction in symptoms following training, with increases in finger temperature of seven to ten degrees Fahrenheit.[3] Biofeedback has shown promising results in helping clients achieve significant reduction in their symptoms without the disagreeable side-effects which often occur with pharmacological or surgical interventions.

Hypertension

Hypertension, or high blood pressure, is a serious disorder which accounts for a large proportion of adult deaths in the U.S. When the cause is not known, the disease is called essential, or idiopathic, hypertension. The medications for hypertension are not free of complications, nor are they effective in all clients. Long term consequences of medications have not been adequately assessed. For this reason, interest in biofeedback as a possible treatment strategy for controlling hypertension has risen in the past several years.

While some researchers and clinicians have used direct blood pressure feedback, many are discovering that teaching handwarming (using feedback) is just as effective. The Biofeedback and Psychophysiological Clinic of the Menninger Foundation has conducted several pioneering studies using skin temperature feedback with hypertensive clients. Its program utilizes thermal biofeedback to assist clients in learning hand and foot warming which produces lasting and significant changes in systolic and diastolic blood pressure as well as EMG feedback to reduce chronic muscle tension. In addition, the program presents more effective stress-management techniques such as altering cognitive interpretations of stressors, time management skills, and more effective communication skills. This comprehensive program also includes: learning diaphragmatic breathing, extensive client education regarding the physiological mechanisms underlying treatment, self-monitoring and charting of blood pressure, and transfer of skills to home or office. Treatment personnel at the Foundation report that eighty-eight percent of their clients with diagnosed hypertension reduce their blood pressure to normal levels and eliminate their medication. The average client achieves normal pressure levels within 20 weeks after beginning treatment. Clearly, this biobehavioral approach shows considerable promise in helping millions of sufferers of high blood pressure cope with their symptoms.[4]

EDUCATIONAL USES FOR BIOFEEDBACK

There are many benefits and uses associated with biofeedback training. Besides the clinical uses described above, biofeedback training can be used for educational purposes. Where clinical training may be seen as a method for reducing or eliminating clinically obvious symptoms of stress-induced disease, educational training focuses on the asymptomatic client who is interested in enhancing his or her ability to cope with current and future stresses. The term asymptomatic can be a tricky one because the absence of symptoms associated with stress-induced disease may be more, or less, in the eye of the client than in the perception of a trained medical professional. Obvious ethical and practical problems develop when a client manifests obvious signs of stress-induced disease but does not see the need for clinical help. As a biofeedback facilitator, it is important to distinguish clinical needs from educational needs. Those clients who may approach biofeedback training for the reduction of specific physiological symptoms should first be diagnosed by a health care professonal. While the client may be referred back to the biofeedback facilitator for stress-induced symptoms, the health care professional must first rule out other, more potentially dangerous, causes for the symptoms. Clients who approach biofeedback training in order to learn about their own psychophysiological processes, or to train their body processes for the control of current or future stressors, can be considered to be learning biofeedback from an educational context.

STRESS MANAGEMENT FOR HEALTHY PEOPLE

Generally speaking, biofeedback training, in an educational mode:

1. enhances a client's awareness of body physiology (validation);
2. aids the client to explore what physiological processes occur with concurrent mind states (validation);
3. aids the client to observe what psychophysiological processes occur due to external stimuli (validation);
4. helps clients to reduce or enhance physiological processes in the bodymind independent of specific external or internal stimuli (training);
5. helps clients to reduce or enhance physiological processes in the bodymind concurrent with specific external or internal stimuli (training).

AWARENESS OF BODY PHYSIOLOGY

With the aid of biofeedback instrumentation clients can learn about their own bodies. A thermal probe can reveal that their hand temperature is not 98.6 degrees Fahrenheit and that their temperature is not constant from one part of the body to another. Just the observation of hand temperature over time can demonstrate that it is in continual flux and is affected by many factors. (More will be said about this later.)

An electromyograph biofeedback instrument provides information about a client's muscle activity, from the simple concepts of muscle contraction to hand movements, to the more complex concepts of muscle contraction symmetry in lower back muscles when bending over to pick up an object. The electromyograph can also point out a lack of muscle specificity when performing particular actions. For example, the everyday process of breathing can be done in a relaxed manner using the diaphragm and intercostal (rib) muscles alone. Yet many people also involve their shoulder and neck muscles, making the breathing process slightly more fatiguing. The awareness of musculature in everyday postural positions (e.g., sitting slouched in a chair versus sitting upright with the spine erect) can be a valuable tool in the education or reeducation of the body.

PHYSIOLOGICAL RESPONSES TO MINDSTATES

Biofeedback instrumentation can also enhance a client's awareness of the physiological responses to particular mind states. Many relaxation techniques function to relax the body via a process involving the psyche. Biofeedback instrumentation can validate many of these relaxation processes. Clients practicing mental imagery techniques or meditation can discover physiological changes that occur during, and as consequences of, their mental activities. It can be very interesting to discover what mental images, ideas, or subjective feelings yield in terms of the individual's physiology. For some, for example, thinking of the last heated argument with a close friend often results in tenser muscles, colder hands, and a raised heart rate. When thinking of a pleasant vacation experience, many individuals demonstrate hand warming, muscle relaxation, and other physiological changes associated with relaxation. It is even fun to explore a variety of subjective mental states to discover how the body responds. Imagining being trapped in a snowbound car, miles from the nearest town, out of gas, with no cars passing by, can help develop cooler hands. The success of comprehending the connections between the mental exercises and the body physiology depends upon the clients ability to visualize and internalize the subjective state to be experienced.

PHYSIOLOGICAL RESPONSES TO EXTERNAL STIMULI

Biofeedback can help individuals understand the role that external stimuli play in altering body physiology. One interesting experiment is to see how the left hand temperature and left forearm muscle tension change when an ice cube is placed on the back of the *right* hand. The cold associated with this external stimuli can generate changes in hand temperature and muscle tension fairly easily. The impact of and response to such stimuli demonstrate how profoundly interconnected the bodymind is to the environment that surrounds it. External stimuli do not have to be physical factors such as an ice cube, a mild pinch, or a gentle massage of tense muscles. They can include sudden startling noises, photographs of bloody accident victims, or comforting reassurances made by others. In other words, verbal, visual, auditory, or other sensed communications have a direct physiological impact on individuals. Research shows that some forms of information yield direct physiological responses in the body even though the information was perceived at a subliminal level of perception.[5] This point argues that the mind and ego do not have to be involved in the *conscious* interpretation of external stimuli for that stimuli to have an effect. Speaking practically, this important point means that we do not have to be consciously aware of external stimuli for them to have a significant impact on our body's physiology.

Of course, the points in the above section point to the fact that external stimuli can also generate changes in the psyche. The changes in the psyche may actually lead to the physiological responses of the individual. Each individual interpretation of the external stimuli plays the leading role in whether (and how) an individual responds. What may be a stress-laden, emotional comment to one individual may be seen as a humorous, somewhat sarcastic quip by another. Our past experiences, current beliefs and expectations, and knowledge all act as filters to aid us in our interpretation of the external environment. How we interpret the external stimuli in our environment has more to do with our physiological response than the external stimuli themselves.

BIOFEEDBACK TRAINING

Biofeedback training can be an educational approach for training *or retraining* each individual's physiology for more situationally appropriate responses to everyday (or specific) stressors. For some individuals, biofeedback training may aid them in learning to increase hand temperature as a means to reach a deeply relaxed state of consciousness. For others, biofeedback training may actually be a retraining of body responses to stressful stimuli, whether generic or specific. For example, if a client tenses certain musculature when taking a major examination or facing a peer review process, the individual's physiology is responding as if the stressor were life threatening. Although such physiological responses are valid in certain circumstances, muscle tensing would probably speed fatigue and make the person function poorly during the examination or review process. As a retraining tool, biofeedback instrumentation would help the individual recognize the sensations of muscle tension and provide practice in learning to relax muscle tension effectively.

TRAINING PHYSIOLOGICAL RESPONSES INDEPENDENT OF STIMULI

Biofeedback training helps clients learn to reduce or enhance physiological body processes in a controlled, comfortable environment. Learning to regulate body physiology takes attentiveness and sensitive exploration to discover the linkages between an individual's psychophysiological state and the biofeedback signal information. The biofeedback facilitator begins and aids this process by providing a quiet, low-stimuli environment that does not add distractions to the client's attending process. Distractions can include extraneous noises, fears about the biofeedback process or instruments, frustrations and worries that the client brought into the training session from home or work, etc. From another perspective, the biofeedback facilitator tries to reduce the noise-to-signal ratio in the client's learning environment. With reduced extraneous, irrelevant information impinging upon the client's perception, the client has an easier time focusing upon and learning from the biofeedback signal and his or her own internal messages.

With a quieter environment, the client can begin to discover what subjective sensations, perceptions, and thoughts are linked to the objective, relevant biofeedback signal provided by instrumentation. Perhaps for one individual the thought of warm blood pulsing rhythmically into the fingertips will aid in increasing hand temperature. For another, focusing on the exhalations of a relaxed, diaphragmatic breathing process will reduce muscle tension in the neck. The actual process of biofeedback training will be discussed in the next chapter.

TRAINING PHYSIOLOGICAL RESPONSES CONCURRENT WITH STIMULI

Biofeedback training must extend beyond the controlled, minimized-stimuli environment, where initial training begins, because the external stimuli of the everyday world of work and life cannot be controlled. From the biofeedback facilitator's perspective, training a client independent of the potential stressors and stimuli of daily life is not realistic. Although it is important to begin training in a controlled environment, clients need to practice their newly acquired skills in a more realistic setting. By moving from a totally controlled environment to one where the biofeedback facilitator adds more and more challenging external stimuli while the client attempts to produce desired physiological changes, training becomes relevant to everyday living. External stimuli from the biofeedback facilitator could range from a simple, suggestive statement (e.g., I'm overworked!, I'm so lonely, Everyone thinks I'm a failure) to actual activities (e.g., listing the client's important work tasks, discussing how lonely the client is, writing down all the client's perceived failings). The ability to regulate body physiology during actual daily events marks the actual success of biofeedback training; the client who is not weaned from the instruments or who can only produce desired physiological changes while in a controlled environment, has not generalized his or her abilities to the conditions where the biofeedback skills are most needed.

The biofeedback facilitator may actually provide assignments for the client to try outside of the safe, controlled training environment. It is through this practice that clients begin to develop and apply their training to more realistic settings.

VALUE OF BIOFEEDBACK INFORMATION IN TRAINING

The signals received from biofeedback instrumentation can be particularly helpful when attempting to alter body physiology. Biofeedback information aids client training when it is: (1) understandable, (2) relevant, (3) accurate, (4) precise, and (5) immediate.

Biofeedback Information in Understandable

The biofeedback facilitator has an important role in explaining and educating clients who use biofeedback instrumentation so that they can comprehend what the signal is saying. When the client understands the biofeedback signal in basic terms, he or she can begin to explore meaningful changes in the signal and how that signal is altered, by the client, during biofeedback training. Understanding how the biofeedback signal relates in basic terms to the goal of the biofeedback training benefits the client who is attempting to make physiological changes.

Biofeedback Information is Relevant

One does not measure height to determine weight loss during a diet. In the same manner, the biofeedback signal must be relevant to the desired changes. When using biofeedback instrumentation to enhance relaxation training, the EMG (electromyograph) provides relevant information for monitoring and reducing muscle tension. Likewise, a thermal biofeedback unit can be used for reducing autonomic nervous system stimulation and enhancing blood flow to the peripheral areas of the body limbs.

Biofeedback Information is Accurate

When learning to alter body physiology through biofeedback instrumentation, valid information is needed to help develop correct links between body physiology and subjective mental states. Invalid information, whether caused by faulty biofeedback sensors, cables, or by instruments that are unreliable, will slow or obstruct biofeedback training. Cheap equipment will not save money if it provides little or invalid information.

Biofeedback Information is Precise

Biofeedback instrumentation is sensitive to small changes in body physiology. For example, electromyograph instruments can measure changes in muscle tension in millionths of a volt. Thermal biofeedback instruments can detect changes in temperature as small as a few hundredths of a degree Fahrenheit. This precision allows clients to begin making those important links between their subjective, internal state and the meaning behind the biofeedback signal. Coarse information cannot provide sensitive enough feedback for clients to know when they are on the right track. To illustrate this point, let's say you're trying to lose weight and are monitoring your progress each morning with a weight scale. But let's also assume that this weight scale registers weight only in increments of ten pounds. For the scale to register *any* weight loss, you must lose *at least ten* pounds. This weight scale may be fine if you have a well delineated diet program with many external motivators to keep you on track. However, if you adopted a self-prescribed dieting strategy that may or may not work for you, and if you need to see some improvement within a couple of weeks in order to continue this diet program you would probably throw out your special weight scale and purchase one that gives more detailed information about weight changes.

The same is true for biofeedback instrumentation. A client may be on the right track when attempting to warm his or her hands but would never know it if the changes were made in tenths of one degree Fahrenheit, and the instrument measured only in full degrees Fahrenheit.

Biofeedback Information is Immediate

Suppose that the previously-mentioned weight scale takes two weeks to process information and give you information. You probably wouldn't keep the scale if it caused that much of a delay in monitoring your progress. The information from the weight scale has value only if it is immediate enough to assist in the perpetuation or alteration of a particular motivated behavior. Likewise, biofeedback information is valuable only if it can demonstrate those physiological effects associated with current mental processes. For example, if a client tries ten different relaxation techniques and only then learns that muscle tension has dropped, what relaxation technique should the client assume led to the positive results? For that matter, it may be a combination of relaxation strategies that had the most beneficial impact. As with many behaviors, immediate feedback, whether from biofeedback instrumentation or the biofeedback specialist, reinforces an individual's behavior.

A MODEL FOR UNDERSTANDING BIOFEEDBACK TRAINING

Figure 13-1 illustrates how biofeedback training works. This model assumes that the behavior of human beings is organized and purposive, and involves a coordinated interaction between perception, cognition, feelings, and behavior. It portrays the relationship of these functions and illustrates biofeedback as the creation of additional pathways of information which modify existing neural and behavioral pathways in more healthful directions.

Figure 13 - 1

Mind-Body Interaction

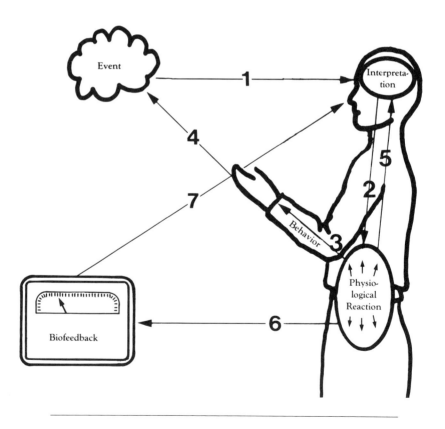

Arrow 1 shows that people experience external events by perceiving them via one or more sensory organs, which transform the events into neural signals, which in turn are relayed to the appropriate centers in the brain. At this point, an important event occurs: the mind interprets the perceived information, i.e., organizes it into meaningful information. One individual can interpret a single event in a multitude of ways, and the specific interpretation is a function of the individual's expectations, past experiences, values, belief systems, and the like. For example, a noise in the basement at night can be interpreted as "someone has broken into the house," or as "the cat got into something," depending on the individual's expectation, experiences, etc. It is important to realize that each particular interpretation carries with it a different physiological reaction or feeling, which is exemplified by Arrow 2. Keep in mind that the events themselves do not cause the feelings we experience. It is not the sound in the basement, but the interpretation of the meaning of that event that creates fear, anxiety, amusement, etc. Since every event can have multiple meanings, and since every meaning or interpretation results in a particular feeling or physiological reaction, it is no wonder that people respond quite differently to the same event. It is important to remember that individuals have direct control over their emotional response to situations through their choice of how they decide to interpret the events which occur in their presence. As far as coping with stress is concerned, individuals have the ability to control their reactions to events that may be appraised as stressful by learning more effective and realistic ways to interpret those events.

Once individuals have chosen a particular interpretation of some event, they will react physiologically in a manner appropriate to that interpretation. For example, if you have interpreted another's behavior towards you as interfering with your purposes, whatever they might be, and you believe that you have the right to do something about it, you very likely will experience anger as the appropriate emotional response to your interpretation. Physiologically, anger is a response which mobilizes a person to meet and overcome events which are perceived as threatening. Fear, on the other hand, is an emotional response designed to enable the organism to escape effectively from a threat which is perceived as overwhelming. While these emotions may differ in some respects physiologically, both appear to be characterized by muscular bracing, increased heart rate and blood pressure, shallow, rapid breathing, sensory alertness, and constriction of the peripheral blood vessels of the hands and feet. It is thought that these, and other responses, are evolutionarily designed to assist the organism in coping with events, whether by "fight or flight," which are perceived as threatening.

In reference to Figure 13-1 one can see that the occurrence of "event-interpretation-physiological reaction (feelings)-behavior constitutes a loop, indicated by Arrows 1, 2, 3, and 4. Human beings, perhaps more than other organisms, have the additional ability to energize Arrows 2 and 3 without the occurrence of some external event (Arrow 1). We are able to create threatening situations by merely symbolizing or visualizing them in our minds. Unfortunately, our bodies are not able to distinguish between a real, external threat and one which is created and visualized mentally. When recalling a past event which caused a great deal of anger or fear, the body may (and actually does) respond with the physiological reactions appropriate to the imagined event. Over a period of time, the sustained physiological arousal can create chronic symptoms of stress - tension headaches, gastrointestinal disorders, cardiovascualr disorders, and others. Human beings also have the ability to rehearse possible negative events of the future, resulting in worry and anxiety: What if I get laid off? What if I can't keep my marriage together? What if my children fall prey to drugs? Thinking about these potential problems can be useful for devising possible methods of coping with these threats when and if they do occur, but many of us engage in needless worry which only serves to exhaust physical reserves, resulting in physiological breakdown.

Not only do we respond to external events (Arrow 1), but we also respond to internal events (Arrow 5). Physical symptoms such as aches and pains, the beating of the heart, stomach contractions, and muscle tension are internal signals which tell us something about the internal functioning of our bodies. The interpretation we attach to these signals is of critical importance. We can interpret these signals in ways which are healthful or that may prove to be destructive. For example, during the work day we notice slightly increased sensations of tension in the neck and shoulder areas. We can ignore these signals (until the pain becomes too severe to ignore!), or we can pay attention to these signals and take measures to reduce the tension by varying posture, engaging in some brief muscle stretching exercises, or even leaving the scene of the stress. The point to remember is that most of us are not as aware as we should be of this pathway associated with Arrow 5 and as a result, by ignoring or misinterpreting these signals, we set the stage for further breakdown.

Biofeedback provides the opportunity to increase our awareness of our internal functioning (Arrow 5) by creating an external loop (Arrows 6 and 7). By plugging in an external channel of information which can detect, amplify, and feed back information about internal physical changes, we can strengthen our internal channels (Arrow 5) and, hence, assume positive control over our internal functioning. In this fashion, biofeedback is an awareness enhancement tool. For example, by using EMG biofeedback regarding changes in muscle tension levels, we can train ourselves to become more internally aware of these muscle changes and learn to control them before it is too late, i.e., before muscle cramping and spasm occurs. Other biofeedback modalities operate in much the same fashion. Using thermal feedback, we can enhance our ability to discriminate minute changes in skin temperature and, hence, achieve increased control over these temperature changes in order to reduce excessive constriction of the blood vessels in the fingers.

CHAPTER 14

BIOFEEDBACK TRAINING:
THE PROCESS

Most professionals consider clinical and educational (health promotion) uses of biofeedback as still in experimental stages of development. As such, there is not a universally accepted training protocol to follow in biofeedback training. Indeed, many biofeedback facilitators believe that the creation of rigid training protocols might inhibit the discovery of new and more effective ways of applying biofeedback principles in helping individuals achieve better control over their stress-related symptoms. Still, a number of guidelines which biofeedback facilitators should be aware of are likely to increase the occurrence of effective learning.

•••••••••• INSTRUCTIONAL POINTERS •••••••

1. The biofeedback training paradigm is a significant departure from the traditional medical model. The biofeedback facilitator should not present himself or herself as the distant, impartial expert who, with superior, mysterious knowledge, is doing something to the client. Rather, the biofeedback facilitator is just that: someone who participates, as a stress management consultant, in the training session with the client; The predominant attitude must be one of "I am here to assist you in becoming more responsible for your health." In addition, the facilitator communicates as one who, with the help of biofeedback instrumentation, assists clients in a learning experience designed to enable them to take over their own training process. Biofeedback is considered, then, a temporary training aid which helps give the clients the tools to carry on their own training in the real world outside the clinic setting.

2. Initially, the clients may perceive themselves as seeking treatment from yet another helping professional and, as such, enter the training environment with essentially a passive, you-heal-me attitude. Throughout the training sessions, the facilitator should keep in mind that the goal then is to enable the client to become a co-participant in the training process. As will be seen later, the adoption of this attitude is essential if clients are to successfully generalize their training outside the walls of the clinic.

3. In biofeedback training, the setting itself exerts a considerable influence over the outcome of the training (as is true in other interventions, be they medical, psychological, or educational). Setting means not only the physical environment but also the personality of the facilitator, either of which will influence for better or worse the impact of the training session. The following section presents more detail about the specific elements of the training environment, including personal variables communicated by the facilitator which may influence the training outcomes.

TRAINING SEQUENCE

This training sequence should be followed for initial sessions with clients who desire to explore biofeedback as an adjunct to learning general stress-management or relaxation skills. It is assumed that these clients do not suffer from significant medical or psychological abnormalities. If such abnormalities do exist, it is essential for the facilitator to have a medical release from the client's current physician. If significant psychological disorders exist, it is essential that the facilitator be in contact with the client's psychologist or counselor before and during the course of the biofeedback experience. In addition, since it is increasingly evident that biofeedback and or relaxation training significantly influence the effects of a wide variety of medications, it is essential that the client's medication dosages be monitored by his or her physician.

INTRODUCTORY PHASE

The client will approach the biofeedback session with a wide variety of expectations which will most certainly affect the course of the training experience. Initially, it is important to ask the client, "What do you wish to gain from biofeedback?" Many clients harbor inappropriate expectations and assumptions that biofeedback will, in a short period of time, miraculously remove their troublesome symptoms; that the machine will heal them by doing something to them; that there will be little effort involved outside the sessions in terms of changing behaviors; or that the biofeedback instruments will somehow enable the facilitator to observe their innermost thoughts and feelings. It is important to assess the presence of these assumptions through careful questioning and by being alert to verbal and nonverbal cues communicated by clients before and during the training sessions.

One way to introduce clients to the experience is by explaining the goals of the session in the following way:

During this introductory training session, I will explain some of the goals of biofeedback, and you will have the opportunity to experiment with one or more types of biofeedback for about 20 to 30 minutes. All I want you to do is use this session to explore some of the connections between the changes registered by the instruments and your internal thoughts and feelings. The instruments are not doing anything *to* you. Biofeedback equipment is much like a set of mirrors that allows you to observe various changes occurring in your muscle tension, skin temperature, or the like. Do not force yourself to relax or to make an effort to elevate your skin temperature. Just relax and observe the variations on the dial. Over the next several weeks you will begin to notice that many of the changes you observe are correlated with certain thoughts and feelings. Once you notice this, you will be in a better position to control the physiological reactions being monitored. What questions do you have about the training so far?

Many facilitators use handouts explaining the nature of biofeedback; these can be useful and can save the facilitator much time. However, never assume that clients' expectations and assumptions about biofeedback training are similar to yours!

TRAINING PHASE

The facilitator should explain every procedure while hooking up the sensors and manipulating the controls on the instrument. This reduces client anxiety and fosters the collaborative atmosphere referred to earlier. To give additionl encouragement that they are involved in the training experience, instruct clients how to regulate the volume and threshold controls (provided the instruments have such controls). Once the client is hooked up, the facilitator should remain at the client's side. An explanation of the physiological mechanisms underlying the stress response can help the client gain an appreciation of how biofeedback will strengthen the relationship denoted by Arrow 5 that was alluded to earlier. (See Figure 13-1, p. 140.) The facilitator may ask a number of questions, including "What do you notice when the needle deflects to the left?" or "What do you suppose happened to cause your finger temperature to drop right now?" Such open-ended questions assist the client to begin building connections between the changes observed in the instruments and his or her own internal physical sensations, thoughts, feelings. In addition, the facilitator may give some suggestions to the client, such as, "Sit back, relax, and begin to think about something coming up next week which causes you anxiety or fear. Hold this image in your mind awhile and begin to notice what physiological changes are occurring to you while you think about this event." As the client visualizes this scene, the facilitator can note fluctuations that do occur on the instruments and comment on these changes as needed. In addition, the facilitator can make comments (give feedback) about physical changes observed in the client while he or she engages in the visualization. For example, "While you imagined that scene I was aware that your breathing became a little more rapid and shallow, and you tensed up your forehead a bit." This sort of feedback helps increase the client's appreciation of how internal mental events affect his or her physiological functioning.

Once the client has had some experience with making these sorts of connections, the facilitator should leave the biofeedback training room and allow the client to continue training on his or her own. Give an instruction, such as, "I will leave you to continue training alone for about 10 to 15 minutes. Continue listening to (or observing) the feedback and notice how the feedback signal varies with what you are thinking and how you are feeling. Are there any questions?" This provides additional opportunities for the client to experiment without the pressure of being watched by the facilitator. In addition, when the facilitator returns to the room, both facilitator and client can observe how the presence of another individual affects the client's physiological response!

DEBRIEFING PHASE

The final phase of training involves discussing what the client has learned from the experience. Once again, asking open-ended questions such as: "What connections did you become aware of between the feedback signals and your thoughts and feelings?" or "What seemed to be occurring internally when the biofeedback signal increased or decreased?" and, finally, "How did this initial experience compare with your expectations?" can help the client assess progress.

The focus of these debriefing questions should be to encourage increased awareness of the mind-body connection, to foster an attitude of curiosity and open-mindedness towards internal physiological events, and to encourage this awareness to extend beyond the training session itself into the client's real world.

HOME PRACTICE

The degree of success in biofeedback training lies in the client's ability to generalize what has been learned in the clinical setting to situations and events outside the clinical setting. Therefore, the facilitator should encourage regular, daily practice in stress management techniques at home and point out that, as with diet programs or exercise, regular observance of the new healthier behaviors is essential for any positive changes to occur. One way to assist the individual, to continue recognizing connections between internal and external events, is to have the client identify cues which occur with some predictability during the day. Such cues might include the ringing of the phone, the beeping of a wristwatch each hour, or the crying of a child. When such identified cues occur, the client should note internal reactions. Another approach is to place signs around the house reminding the individual to look inward and note signs of excessive muscle bracing, constricted breathing, or other physiological signs of stress. At these times, the client should practice a brief unstressing procedure or relaxation technique as outlined elsewhere in this book.

Keeping a daily log of events that cause a general stress reaction is an additional technique for increasing awareness of the stress response. A spouse or roommate could assist by pointing out external signs that indicate a stress reaction is occurring. Once the client develops awareness of how the body responds to various stressors in his or her environment, this awareness will begin to occur automatically. For example, if each time an internal scan of your stress level revealed a clenched jaw, soon the increased jaw tension in itself will serve as a cue to focus attention inward and engage in an unstressing maneuver. The ultimate goal of biofeedback training (as far as this particular example is concerned) is to train the jaw muscle to remain relaxed throughout the situations which originally led to the increased muscle tension.

The overall training sequence for biofeedback is like any reeducational approach. It is assumed that clients are not as aware as they could be regarding internal functioning, or, more exactly, in making connections between internal physiological functioning and external events. Biofeedback-assisted stress management, then, seeks to teach a renewed awareness of these connections and relationships and to encourage a conscious practice of the new responses in real-life situations that will allow the new responses to become automatic, that is, a part of the client's natural functioning.

FORMS OF BIOFEEDBACK TRAINING
AND USES FOR RELAXATION

EMG (ELECTROMYOGRAPHIC) BIOFEEDBACK

EMG biofeedback is the process of monitoring changes in muscle tension and relaying these changes to the client in the form of varying tones, lights, or pointers on a dial. With this external information available, the client can dramatically increase his or her awareness of the varying levels of muscle tension. From a stress management point of view, the client becomes increasingly able to note these changes and control them before excessively elevated levels occur resulting in tension-related muscle pain or soreness. Typical sensor placements for stress management include the frontalis (forehead) muscle which registers the summed levels of contraction of the muscles of the scalp, face, and jaw; the trapezius (upper back) muscle group; the forearm flexor muscle group; the thoracic and lumbar paraspinal muscles (for those with excessive muscle tension in the back); and the masseter (jaw) muscle. Obviously, tension levels in any muscle group located near the surface of the skin can be monitored and fed back to the client for the purposes of increasing awareness of what the muscles are doing.

Muscular Dysponesis

Before exploring the uses of muscle tension biofeedback, it is important to be aware of how inappropriate muscle tension interferes with healthy functioning of the bodymind. Dysponesis, from the Greek *dys*, meaning bad, and *ponesis*, meaning effort or exertion, refers to misplaced efforts. For example, while negotiating heavy traffic you may find your shoulders excessively tightened and your jaw clenched. This misplaced effort contributes nothing to the successful execution of the task at hand, namely, safe negotiation through the traffic. In fact, this excessive, misplaced muscle tension may actually interfere with the completion of the task. Other examples of this inappropriate muscle tension are hunching one's shoulders while typing, excessively squeezing one's ski poles while cross-country skiing, or contracting one's throat excessively while reading (subvocalization).

EMG biofeedback can be used to illustrate dysponesis to the client. For example, EMG sensors attached to the pectoralis (chest) muscles reveal how much these muscles are used in the act of breathing. Many individuals have learned inadvertently to use these upper body muscles to assist them in the act of inspiration rather than letting the diaphragm and intercostal (rib) muscles carry out the task. As such, their breathing patterns become shallow and localized in the thorax. EMG biofeedback, in this case, allows clients to learn how they can inhale without involving the muscles of the upper thorax—a dysponetic act.

By attaching the sensors to the muscles of the forearm, one can discover additional examples of dysponetic activity. To determine the extent to which a client has learned specificity of muscle effort, ask him or her to make a tight fist while monitoring the muscles of the *opposite* arm. If the EMG indicator shows a significant increase in muscle tension in the opposite arm, it is likely that the client is predisposed to use unnecessary muscles in other activities he or she engages in. When given feedback of this activity, the individual can learn to tighten up the muscles of one arm while keeping the opposite arm relaxed. This type of EMG feedback has many potential applications, especially in the area of athletics. It is likely that many athletes exhibit muscle tension in muscle groups which are not directly involved in the athletic activity, resulting in unnecessary fatigue.

Another example involves attaching the sensors to the muscles surrounding the voice box. Many individuals engage in the dysponetic activity of subvocalization while reading silently, which results in unnecessary fatigue and soreness around the voice box. EMG feedback in this example provides immediate information related to this misdirected effort so that the client can learn to control the muscle activity. With appropriate switches, it is possible to connect a reading lamp directly to the EMG feedback device, thus requiring the client to maintain low EMG levels while reading. As soon as the EMG level surpasses a preset threshold, the reading lamp turns off and the client is unable to continue reading.

To illustrate another example of discovering and redirecting dysponetic activity, have the biofeedback client imagine a series of arousing scenes, such as a past experience which resulted in anger, fear, anxiety, etc. By observing the relevant EMG indices, the client can become aware of the intimate connection between mental images and physical reactions. This exercise clearly presents evidence that the body responds to imaginary stimuli in much the same manner that it responds to real external stimuli. If the body responds in this manner to fleeting memories and images, how much more it must react to our omnipresent thoughts and reactions to events which occur in daily life! Experiments such as these provide extremely important evidence for the intimate connections between mind and body.

As an adjunct to relaxation training, EMG biofeedback can provide immediate information about how much progress the client is making regarding relaxation. Many individuals who have lost their awareness of muscle tension levels may erroneously believe they are relaxed when the EMG readings indicate that actual muscle tension levels remain elevated. It is almost as if the chronically-elevated muscle tension masks the variations in muscle tension levels, making it difficult for the client to notice the variations. Armed with accurate feedback as to the real muscle tension fluctuations, the client can begin to become aware of the small variations in muscle tension and, as a result, begin to lower them to more appropriate levels of functioning.

EMG biofeedback is a useful adjunct for relaxation training for many individuals and may be an essential component for others who are unable to sense the variations in muscle tension. EMG biofeedback is also in widespread clinical use and is being applied in the treatment of tension headaches, TMJ syndrome and bruxism, anxiety, insomnia, neural disorders such as spasmodic torticollis, and a wide variety of other symptoms and disorders where excessive or inappropriate levels of muscle tension play a major role. EMG biofeedback also plays a significant role in rehabilitation and muscle re-education where feedback indicating very low levels of muscle activity is necessary for the client to learn the reuse of a particular muscle. Many textbooks and articles summarize these clinical applications.[1]

THERMAL BIOFEEDBACK

Biofeedback instrumentation can detect minute changes of temperature that occur on or within the human body. These temperature changes, when controlled for extraneous factors, reflect alterations of blood flow within the client's circulatory system near the biofeedback unit's sensor. Whether the sensor is located on the client's right middle finger tip, left great toe, or right earlobe, the biofeedback unit's sensor is heated from the warm blood pumped to that area by the heart. Now if the arterioles and capillaries of the body area near the sensor are constricted and carrying little warm blood, the area would probably feel cool and clammy to the touch. The thermal biofeedback unit would register the body area as lower in temperature. If the arterioles and capillaries are dilated and carrying a plentiful amount of warm blood, the area would feel warm or hot. The thermal biofeedback unit would register the body area as higher in temperature. Thus, thermal biofeedback training is of practical importance when attempting to alter blood flow to body areas.

The psychophysical connection between mental processes and blood flow is complex. Basically, however, as an individual tenses, the autonomic nervous system increases the amount of stimulation to the sympathetic neural pathways throughout the body. The sympathetic neural pathway maintains a basic amount of stimulation to the muscles within the walls of the body's arterioles, preventing their total dilation. A normal amount of neural stimulation to the arteriolar muscles is normal and desirable, but, when anxiety and tension produce an excessive stimulation of these neural pathways, arteriolar constriction can shut down the flow of blood to the area. In some areas and under certain conditions arteriolar constriction can be severe. The result, cold hands, is one symptom of this greater sympathetic nervous system stimulation.

As an individual relaxes and becomes physiologically calm, the amount of normal neural stimulation to the sympathetic nervous system decreases slightly. This reduction in sympathetic nervous system tone allows the arteriolar muscles that control blood vessel diameter to relax more, expanding the arteriolar diameter and allowing more warm blood to course into the area. The result, warm hands, represents decreased sympathetic nervous system stimulation, and also indicates a more relaxed body condition.

"Cold hands, warm heart" may be true at an esthetic level, but cold hands typically indicate a stimulated nervous system at the psychophysical level. There are, however, factors that can influence the correct interpretation of thermal biofeedback information, and it would be worthwhile to explore them.

• • • • • • • • • INSTRUCTIONAL POINTERS • • • • • • • •

1. *The majority of the environment around a warm human body is cooler or warmer than the body itself. Putting one's hand, with a thermal biofeedback sensor attached, onto a desktop will most likely result in a thermal biofeedback signal that measures the average temperature of the client's hand and the desktop. Placing cool hands in one's lap so that the thermal biofeedback sensor rests against the client's warm thigh will probably yield the averaged temperature of the client's finger and thigh. Moving the body part (and* attached sensor) through the air will again yield an averaged temperature: that of the flowing air and the body part. Instead of moving the body part through still air, the same result can be achieved by moving air (a draft) across the quiet body part with the attached thermal sensor.

The thermal biofeedback sensor always integrates the information from environmental objects around the sensor, whether they be a fingertip, desk, or room air. The client or biofeedback facilitator should realize this fact and minimize any change in non-body environments so that the information from the sensor meaningfully represents changes in the client's body alone.

2. It is important to properly connect the thermal biofeedback sensor to the chosen body area. Many biofeedback units have Velcro strips to attach the sensor to a client's finger or toe. If the strips are attached too tightly or loosely they can reduce the validity of the thermal biofeedback signal. A Velcro strip (or piece of tape) that is too tightly wrapped around a finger or toe can impede blood flow to the body area and give the false impression that the area is not getting warmer. A Velcro strip wrapped too loosely may allow air currents to flow across the sensor, or it may allow the thermal sensor to move about and produce a fluctuating temperature.

A square or rectangular piece of dense tape is a better connector for the thermal sensor. The tape would not have to wrap all the way around a finger or toe, and it would help prevent the thermal sensor from making variable contact with the body area.

3.   A change in absolute hand temperature can be deceiving. Just because a person can increase hand temperature by only 3 degrees does not mean that the client is not as good as someone else who can increase hand temperature by 15 degrees. The "Law of Initial Values" applies here because when hand temperature is already very warm, it can't get much warmer. While hands that start at 69 degrees Fahrenheit can climb into the 90's, hands that start at 92 can only climb a few degrees.

Research demonstrates as significant an amount of vasodilation with a small temperature change (92 to 94 degrees F) as with a larger temperature change that starts at a lower temperature (69 to 88 degrees F).

Relaxation Training With Thermal Biofeedback

The first step in thermal biofeedback training is to determine the baseline temperature of a body area. With a thermal biofeedback sensor in place, the client can determine his or her temperature and what sensations of coolness or warmth correlate with the biofeedback signal. The biofeedback facilitator should also explain how to decipher the signals given by the lights, meters, and digital outputs, (i.e., "That's my finger temperature: 78.9 degrees Fahrenheit - my fingers feel cool!").

Next the client should build connections between psychophysiological states of the mindbody and the biofeedback information. The biofeedback facilitator may lead the client through a visualization technique or have the client focus on sensations of warmth and heaviness in the sensor's area. The facilitator may use autogenic phrases, progressive relaxation techniques, or a concentrative meditation technique to help the client reach a deeply relaxed state. Whatever the strategy, after the relaxation technique is over, the client should objectively observe the impact a specific relaxation technique has had on his or her hand temperature (and, consequently, nervous system) as a general indication of relaxation.[2]

Another way, however, to relax the bodymind is to directly attend to the biofeedback signal and *will* it to change upwards. Some people have this skill - to alter hand temperature merely by willing the biofeedback signal to change - and can produce exciting results of temperature shift.

A more nondirective approach is to ask the client to explore subjective thoughts, feelings, and sensations he or she thinks would help produce deep relaxation. Each person can probably recollect a mental private place that is a brief respite from the busy, stressful world. Going to that private place may help the client feel calm and relaxed, and may generate a physiologically relaxed state in the individual as evidenced by the thermal biofeedback signal.

DERMAL BIOFEEDBACK

Like thermal biofeedback, dermal biofeedback monitors autonomic nervous system changes occuring in the body. Theoretically, dermal biofeedback can be divided into two groups: skin potential responses (SPR) to psychophysiological stimuli, and skin conductance responses (GSR or SC) to psychophysiological stimuli. There are subtle differences between the two, but the details associated with the differences are more appropriately covered within biofeedback textbooks. Practically speaking, however, the two dermal responses monitor similar physiological changes in the skin and can, therefore, be discussed together.

The dermal responses to psychophysiological stimuli appear to be related to changes in the secretory sweat glands located within the skin. The sweat glands of the skin normally produce sweat throughout the day, but the experience of wet, clammy skin usually occurs only when an individual is involved in exercise or a strong, sudden stressor. People are not aware of perspiration at normal levels of sweating because it evaporates quickly upon reaching the skin surface. However, when an individual is exposed to a stressor, the autonomic nervous system stimulates sweat glands to secrete at a rate higher than normal. This increase in sweat also changes the electrical characteristics of the skin. With more electrolyte (salty sweat) just below and on the surface of the skin, the skin is less resistant to a small current of electricity. It is possible to detect these changes in the skin with a Galvanic Skin Response (GSR) device that measures the resistance of the skin to a microampere current. When the skin conducts current more easily, the GSR device translates the lowered resistance into a biofeedback signal that aids psychophysical changes.

The dermal response is one of the most sensitive and rapid in biofeedback training. It is possible to generate dermal responses with such simple activities as calling the person's name or merely suggesting the application of a stressor. Snapping one's fingers right in front of the client's face is enough to generate a dermal response that can be seen on a dermal biofeedback unit. One of the author's favorite methods of eliciting a dermal response is to tell the client: "Now I'm going to ask you a very personal question about a most embarrassing topic. . . ." The sentence rarely has to be completed; the question never has to be asked. The client's response to the intimacy that he or she may have to share in answering the not-yet-asked question is enough to elicit a dermal response.

Dermal Biofeedback in Relaxation Training

In relaxation training, dermal biofeedback can: (1) help the biofeedback facilitator by monitoring phrases, words, and tactics that work well or poorly for a client; (2) enhance the training as the individual monitors his or her level of autonomic nervous system stimulation; and (3) provide information concerning a stressor that allows gradual desensitization.

Unlike thermal biofeedback, dermal biofeedback provides much more immediate information about the effects of thoughts and feelings on bodymind physiology. For example, as discussed in Chapter 3, some words are inappropriate for relaxing certain clients, like using the word "heavy" when attempting to relax a very obese person. With dermal biofeedback, the facilitator can monitor reactions to specific relaxation words or tactics by watching changes in dermal response during training. Subtle changes in dermal biofeedback cue the facilitator when phrases and words are having a relaxing effect and when they may not be beneficial for the client. Caution must be used, however, when interpreting the dermal biofeedback signal: Words or comments said by the relaxation facilitator may not be directly linked to each thought and physiological reaction of the client. Changes in breathing and in level of mental alertness may alter the dermal response even though the relaxation facilitator is using appropriate phrases to relax clients.

Just like the thermal and EMG biofeedback instruments, dermal biofeedback units help clients learn to relax. By heeding the dermal feedback signal, clients can begin to alter body physiology, or they can discover how the body responds to relaxation strategies like autogenic phrases, progressive relaxation, a concentrative meditation, or the like. However, dermal biofeedback is much more reactive than the other major forms of biofeedback. Merely watching the dermal biofeedback signal change can be enough stimulus to cause further dermal changes, leading to even further signal changes. This positive feedback loop can be stressful to some individuals who perceive themselves getting more and more anxious as they watch the dermal biofeedback unit. Such anxiety about the growing positive feedback loop can be enough to bring it about: a physiological self-fulfilling prophecy. Of course, once this begins to happen the facilitator should break the loop early by turning the device away so that the visual feedback no longer reaches the client, or turning off the sound so that the auditory feedback does not generate client anxiety.

The third use for dermal biofeedback, desensitization to a stressor, should be considered carefully. Some people react to stressors because of personal beliefs or past experiences that should only be explored and enhanced by a trained counselor or psychologist. If the stressor and the client's response to the stressor does not appear to be out of the ordinary, dermal biofeedback can be used to reduce the severity of physiological response to the stressor. Gradually increased exposure to the stressor that provides time for the client to adapt to the current level of the stressor can allow the client to eventually feel comfortable in the presence of the full stressor. The exact details of this process are beyond the scope of this introductory chapter.

OTHER BIOFEEDBACK APPLICATIONS

Heart Rate

When individuals are given beat-to-beat feedback of heart rate, they can learn to voluntarily increase and decrease their heartrate. There have been several methods, both direct and indirect, for giving heart rate feedback to clients. One of the earliest approaches simply allowed clients to observe moment-to-moment fluctuations in their heart rate as they listened through a stethoscope. Newer devices measure the beat-to-beat time and compute an overall heart rate, which is fed back to clients as a digital readout. Other approaches measure the time a pulse wave takes to pass two locations on the artery supplying blood to the arm and hand. These direct methods, however, are not essential for training individuals to learn control over heart rate. Indirect methods such as EMG or muscle tension feedback have also helped individuals achieve control over heart rate. Clinically, most intervention programs are designed to train clients to lower abnormally fast heart rates to more acceptable levels.[3]

EEG (Brain Wave) Biofeedback

Experiments carried out in the late 1950's by Kamiya indicated that individuals can be trained to control their alpha rhythm. Alpha rhythm is a brain wave frequency occurring in the brain at 8 to 12 Hertz (cycles per second). It has been dubbed the idling frequency since it tends to be suppressed when the individual is engaged in any cognitive task requiring attention. Although many clinicians and researchers associated the alpha rhythm with a calm, relaxed, but alert state of mind, there is considerable disagreement about what types of subjective experiences are associated with alpha waves. Biofeedback has been carried out with other brain wave rhythms: theta (4-8 Hertz), beta (13-20 Hertz), and fast beta (40-50 Hertz). Different mental states have been associated with these brain wave frequencies. Theta waves seem to accompany drowsy, dream-like states. Individuals often report that they are engaging in vivid mental images or intense daydreaming. Some clinicians have found that providing theta wave feedback can help individuals suffering from certain forms of insomnia. Beta waves are associated with alertness and attentiveness as well as anxiety and tension; fast beta waves are associated with vigilance and concentration. With appropriate feedback of desired brain waves, individuals can be trained to increase or suppress these wave patterns.

However, due to difficulties in the detection of EEG waves and the presence of spurious sources of similar Hertz waves, EEG feedback has not found as useful a place in the stress-management clinic as EMG, dermal, and thermal devices. Perhaps the most useful clinical application of EEG biofeedback has been in the treatment of certain types of epilepsy. Some individuals have learned to reduce the frequency and severity of their seizures by learning to suppress certain brainwave patterns associated with these seizures.[4]

CHAPTER 15

PRACTICAL RELAXATION TECHNIQUES

Once clients have mastered the basic relaxation techniques of proper body position, sensory awareness training, breathing rhythm techniques and total body relaxation, they are ready for more practical forms of relaxation. These more practical relaxation techniques focus on how clients can make relaxation a daily function even when five minutes or more of total seclusion are not possible or feasible. This chapter discusses these practical relaxation techniques, their benefits, their diversity, and specific examples of their usefulness.

Practical relaxation techniques are just that - a group of techniques that can be used in the practical manner in which people live their lives. These techniques are short in duration, usually requiring less than one minute to perform; they are designed to be implemented during the day without the luxury of a plush chair or quiet environment; and they are an extension of a basic relaxation training program. As an extension of a basic program, the facilitator needs to recognize that practical relaxation techniques utilize previously learned and practiced skills. For these reasons, practical relaxation techniques are most effective when they are used to supplement a basic relaxation training program.

Unlike total body relaxation techniques that are performed once or twice each day for five to twenty minutes, practical relaxation techniques are meant to be used frequently and regularly throughout the day as needed. These short, frequent sessions enhance sensory awareness and provide frequent feedback about tension levels throughout the body. In a way, these techniques enable the body to function as a biofeedback machine. Using the information gained about tension levels, clients can select a brief relaxation technique to reduce or eliminate this unwanted, and usually fatiguing, tension. These small, subtle changes made frequently throughout the day establish (or re-establish) mind-body pathways that respond to life events and hassles in a more relaxed, effective manner.

Obviously, practical relaxation techniques do not provide the same mental or physiological benefits as deep relaxation techniques. Rather, this group of techniques provides other benefits which contribute to managing the frequency and/or intensity of the stress response. The facilitator should always keep in mind that clients need to determine the specific outcome desired when utilizing practical relaxation techniques. In general, however, benefits of practical relaxation techniques include: (1) *consciously* raising awareness of tension levels, or other irritations or symptoms, in the body from too much stress; (2) *consciously* and quickly reducing unnecessary tension or serving as a cue to perform a total body relaxation technique; (3) conserving the expenditure of body energy, thus reducing physical and mental fatigue; (4) being quick and easy to do at any time or location during the day.[1]

Several visualization techniques were mentioned in the basic relaxation program (see Chapter 11). Many of those imagery techniques could be considered practical relaxation techniques. In addition to those, Differential Relaxation and Brief Relaxation techniques meet the description and criteria of practical relaxation techniques. Each can be a practical vehicle for establishing and maintaining a healthier mind-body balance.

DIFFERENTIAL RELAXATION

Differential relaxation describes the group of techniques that differentiate muscle sense. During a basic relaxation program, use progressive relaxation or sensory awareness techniques to develop muscle sense. Once clients are able to recognize muscle tension and relaxation, they can use the relaxed muscles to assist the whole body to let go and relax. Here, differential relaxation "involves learning to differentiate between muscle tensions required to perform a particular task and muscle tensions that are not needed for that task."[2] (You may want to refer to the section on muscular dysponesis in Chapter 14 for further understanding of selectively differentiating muscle use.)

For our discussion in this chapter, let's suppose you have these five clients in your basic relaxation program:

John is a tool and die maker who spends the majority of each working day at his machine producing parts that require one-sixtyfourth precision to specification.

Jackie is an advertising and marketing executive who spends much of her work day in meetings or interviews with potential clients.

Jay is a university professor who spends the majority of each day behind a desk engaged in various writing tasks—grading essays, summarizing meetings, authoring lesson plans and developing research articles for publication.

Martha is a long distance trucker who frequently spends 12 to 14 hours behind the steering wheel.

Ellen is a pediatrician with a heavy, and usually over-booked, patient load. She races between offices to see patients and is frequently interrupted by other staff or items needing her attention.

Each of these individuals tells you that they are mentally or physically fatigued before their respective work days end. With a little probing you discover more information about factors contributing to their tension levels. John's early fatigue might be due to improper alignment of the body as he constantly shifts weight from one foot to another, slouches over his machine, and clenches his jaw during specific movements with his hands; Jackie's early fatigue may come from shifting her weight from one buttocks to another, crossing legs, and squinting her eyes while listening; Jay's early fatigue may come from squeezing the pen when writing for more than twenty minutes, putting extra pressure on the paper with his non-writing hand, and squeezing shoulder muscles together as he leans closer to his work; Martha reports an increase of gripping-type pressure on the steering wheel over time which seems to generalize to her jaws after several hours; and Ellen recounts frustration and mental fatigue from rushing into and out of offices, feverishly scanning patient records in the process, or trying to focus on the other items which creep in between.

Diversity such as this gives the facilitator an excellent opportunity to discuss differential relaxation in general or provide specific examples of how each person can develop differential relaxation techniques for periodic daily use.[3] Eventually, these techniques can be used to assess tension levels in muscle groups that are not contributing to the task at hand or to relax these muscle groups.

•••••••• INSTRUCTIONAL POINTERS ••••••••

1.   *Some clients may have difficulty in conceptualizing how different muscle groups do or don't contribute to a specific task. To demonstrate this have clients work in pairs. Have one client write a short paragraph about any topic while the other client picks up the non-writing hand by the index and middle fingers. The client holding the fingers (in a manner that frees the whole arm from the supporting environment) should move the hand sideways and in small circles until it is free of muscle tension - all while the partner is writing the paragraph. Since these demonstrations aid most clients to experience muscle differentiation, you may want to develop a series of demonstrations using different muscle groups of the body.*

2. Since practical relaxation techniques are based upon the foundations of the basic program, have clients actually perform differential relaxation techniques during the remainder of the class. For example: have clients use proper posture that allows them to be mentally alert and relaxed for lectures, films, or discussions; periodically have clients check the pressure they are placing on the pen or pencil, or in their jaws, while taking notes; have clients stand on the exhalation phase of the breathing rhythm and then move in tune with the exhalations during their breaks. With proper planning and scheduling, you can work many of these techniques into the last portions of your class.

BRIEF RELAXATION

Another group of practical relaxation techniques, called brief relaxation techniques, can supplement a basic relaxation program. Brief means brief; most of these techniques involve a maximum of five complete breathing cycles. These techniques generally assist individuals in modifying their response to the external environment. The external stimulus serves as a cue to use the breathing mechanism, first, to relax and, then, to respond in a slower, calmer manner.

The telephone is a good example of an external cue since most people are conditioned to answer it as soon as it starts ringing. When using the ringing of a telephone as the stimulus, the client would, first, perform a brief relaxation technique (such as the R and R technique described below) and, then, answer the phone. It's important to understand that brief relaxation techniques re-condition clients' normal response patterns. The immediate results (relaxation) come from performing the technique while the long range results (responding in a slower, calmer manner) come from practicing these techniques over time.

The following examples of brief relaxation techniques are not presented in any specific order or sequence. The facilitator should suggest how and when these techniques could be incorporated into regular, daily schedules.

R AND R TECHNIQUE (RELAX AND RESPOND)

The R and R is a two-breath tension-control technique that can be done in five to fifteen seconds. The first exhalation is the relaxation portion while the second exhalation is the responding phase.

The relaxation breath: Take a deep breath and, as you exhale, allow the body to relax, sink down and become comfortably heavy.

The respond breath: Take in a second breath and, as you exhale, respond (i.e., return to your previous activity; for example, answer the telephone).

If time permits, you may want to repeat the first breath several times before the respond breath. If you do, be sure to use a normal breath on successive inhalations.[4]

TRIANGULAR BREATHING

In a relaxed position, with eyes open or closed, inhale fully to a count of 5; hold the breath to a count of 5; then exhale slowly and completely to a count of 7. For the next two or three breathing cycles, focus on the exhalations and allow various muscles to let go and relax. When ready, resume normal activity.

QUIETING RESPONSE

In a relaxed position, allow your eyes to close. Take *one* inhalation and scan the body for noticeable tension. On the exhalation, visualize blowing the tension out of the body. Breathe in normally and, on this exhalation, repeat silently, "I am at peace, relaxed."[5]

QR GENERALIZATION EXERCISE

In a relaxed position with closed eyes use a count of 1-2-3-4 to:

Breathe out through your magic breathing holes;

Breathe in through your magic breathing holes;

Let your jaw go loose and breathe out through your magic breathing holes.[6]

•••••••• INSTRUCTIONAL POINTERS ••••••••

1. *As simple as these techniques seem, clients should practice several of them once or twice prior to leaving your class session. It's important to monitor clients so they don't deep-breathe more than two breathing cycles or force the breathing rhythm. Discuss ways these techniques can be incorporated into daily schedules* at least ten times each day.

2. *These techniques promote readiness for longer relaxation techniques. Encourage clients to share how they plan to use, or have used, these techniques. Their suggestions and techniques can be good examples and can broaden your repertoire of brief relaxation techniques.*

CHAPTER 16

ASSESSING AND EVALUATING CLIENT ABILITIES IN STRESS MANAGEMENT

Assessing someone's ability to manage stress is a difficult process. Many variables have an impact upon the client's ability: his or her perception of the internal and external environment, previous specific training, internal motivation to attempt stress management activities, and genetic and biological variables that cannot be altered. Because all of these variables can modify an individual's stress reaction, it is difficult to determine an individual's ability to manage stress. However, this chapter explores strategies for assessing and evaluating a client's ability to handle stress. With this collection of strategies, the facilitator may be able to determine a client's stress management capabilities.

CAVEATS: MEASURING STRESS RESPONSES IN A LEARNING ENVIRONMENT

Stress management skills in a learning environment are different from those in a real world environment. Observing and measuring clients involved in a relaxation workshop will be different from observing people in a more stressful, workday situation.

First and foremost, relaxation programs train clients how to relax in a controlled, low stimuli environment. This is entirely appropriate when learning how to relax. However, the relaxation skills cannot be applied effectively to everyday life unless conditions that more closely approximate the real world are introduced into the training sessions.

Secondly, a relaxation training program often makes clients more aware of physiological stimuli that act as cues to the stress reactions; but clients may not recognize these cues as easily in the real world. Trainers of relaxation techniques point out cues to both the stress and relaxation response but don't always train the clients in ways to cue themselves. In other words, the learning environment of the relaxation training program helps participants explore relaxation techniques with the aid and guidance of the relaxation facilitators. *Unless the relaxation facilitators teach relaxation skills that progress through a variety of stimuli, subjects may not be able to correctly cue themselves in the real world setting.*

Thirdly, workshops often teach a series of relaxation techniques, allowing the beneficial effects of the first and second techniques to enhance a third or fourth relaxation strategy. In "multiple treatment interaction," the observed benefits of one relaxation technique may actually be the benefits accrued from two techniques done one after the other or the benefits accrued from the two techniques enhancing each other. It is difficult to surpass a full day of relaxation, especially when the stressors and environment are controlled by the facilitator. Please keep in mind that most clients will not have the time in a busy schedule of activities, or even at the end of a day, to practice three or more different relaxation techniques in a row. Practicing different relaxation techniques is important; but selecting the most beneficial ones is more important.

PHYSIOLOGICAL REACTIONS

One way to determine a client's reactions to stressors and relaxation strategies is to measure them. Measurements, taken with the aid of biofeedback instrumentation, can objectively demonstrate the physiological conditions of a client. Physiological measurements can be taken to: (1) establish a baseline, (2) observe changes during relaxation attempts, and (3) observe reactions to psychological and physical stressors.

BASELINE OBSERVATIONS

To determine a baseline, i.e., a condition unaffected by attempts to relax or by induced stressors, biofeedback instrumentation can measure basic muscle tension levels, hand temperature, skin conductance, heart rate, and other measures of a client's physiology. However, there may be problems in determining a baseline. The individual may have been exposed to a stressor, such as a brief argument, just prior to baseline measurement. Or perhaps he or she has just run five miles and has an elevated metabolism that would skew the measurements. For that matter, being hooked up to the biofeedback instrument could be a stressor, especially if the client has any performance anxiety associated with the collection and recording of baseline measures. The client may become more stressed during the recording of baseline measures. In other words, the collection of physiological data through biofeedback instrumentation can alter the physiological processes within the individual.

One major problem is that individual body physiology naturally fluctuates during the day. It is hard to determine when, or when not, to take measurements that can be considered normal for an individual. A measurement taken during the first few waking minutes of the day can be altered if the individual dreamed of a pleasant experience or had a nightmare. And within each individual there are circadian, lunar, and other rhythms of differing physiological measures.

Another major problem is the difficulty of standardizing biofeedback application procedures. Both EMG and GSR biofeedback devices have feedback signals which can vary considerably depending upon where the sensors are placed, how the sensors are attached, and how long the sensors stay attached. Although thermal and heart rate biofeedback modalities are more stable when applied at the same body site, problems still exist.

In light of all the extraneous variables that have an impact upon baseline measures, it is wise to use them with extreme caution. If baseline measurements are taken, allow fifteen to twenty minutes for client stabilization before actually collecting data. If multiple measures are taken of one individual at different times, be certain to keep as many environmental conditions (room, temperature, humidity, lighting, time of the day, day of the week) the same as is posible.

Also, one client's baseline should not be compared to another client's baseline. Interclient variability can be great due to many variables other than a client's skill in relaxation and reactivity to stressors. The fat content of the skin, the normal level of autonomic nervous system stimulation, the genetically-coded neural brain pattern of an individual, the circulatory system idiosyncrasies, and a lifetime of lifestyle choices are all factors and valid reasons why one client's biofeedback signal does not start at the same baseline as other clients' signals.

OBSERVATIONS DURING RELAXATION ATTEMPTS

As an individual relaxes many physiological changes can occur. When attempts to look at baseline measures may be confounded by many extraneous variables, physiological changes during the client's attempts to relax can be easier to interpret. There are still problems, but they are easier to handle.

As a client is instructed to relax, the biofeedback facilitator can look for beneficial changes in biofeedback signals: an increase in hand temperature, a decrease in skin conductance, a decrease in EMG signal, a drop in heart rate, etc. Such changes are correlated with subjective experiences of moderate or deep relaxation and can be helpful in assessing a client's ability to relax. Change scores, i.e., the change in a biofeedback signal between the beginning and the end of the relaxation period, can give an indirect measure of ability to relax in a controlled environment. Comparing client change scores between clients is still not appropriate, but the comparison begins to give a better estimate of ability to relax without a stressor present.

However, there are still some problems associated with change scores generated during a relaxation training. First of all, certain stressors may still be present even though the client is attempting to relax. Performance anxiety, especially if the client wants to perform well in front of the biofeedback facilitator, can be a strong factor in preventing relaxation for some clients, while it may be a weak factor for others. Some individual stressors, even when the client is instructed to relax, can be very persistent and prevent the client from truly giving complete attention to the relaxation task at hand. Another difficulty in interclient and intraclient comparisons is the Law of Initial Values. Practically speaking, if one's hands are already 93 degrees Fahrenheit, it is difficult to expect more than a few degrees of change; however, if one's hands are at 78 degrees Fahrenheit, a large change in hand temperature is possible.

There are ways to attempt to control, or at least measure, these confounding variables. Applying the Law of Initial Values, it is possible to use the beginning value as a covariate for the end value of the biofeedback signal. Many statistical techniques can then look at end values of the biofeedback signal to see what changes have occurred, with the effect of the initial value taken out.

With other stressors confounding relaxation attempts, it is important to try to observe their presence if clients cannot get rid of them. Of course the biofeedback facilitator should try to reduce performance anxiety by making the client feel comfortable in the relaxation environment. The suggestion: "Don't force yourself to relax, just allow your body to relax as it naturally can," may help generate a correct mental attitude for the experience. The biofeedback facilitator should let the client know that the results of the client's relaxation assessment will not surprise nor disappoint the facilitator.

ASSESSMENT WITH PSYCHOLOGICAL AND PHYSICAL STRESSORS

Assessment during relaxation attempts may give a perspective of the capabilities of a client in a controlled environment; but an assessment of a client's ability to withstand stressors is probably most akin to measuring capabilities practical for real world situations.

Instead of watching biofeedback signals to see how well a client can warm fingertips or reduce muscle tension while relaxing, this strategy focuses on how well a client can reduce the body's stress response in the presence of, or immediately after, a mild stressor. Again, problems of interpretation crop up because the client's interpretation of the stressor has much to do with a client's reaction to the stressor.

Stressors can be arbitrarily divided into two groups: psychological and physical. The main distinction between the two is that psychological stressors depend heavily upon the interpretation of the individual being stressed, while physical stressors are known to have significant physical impacts that are stressful. These distinctions do not mean that physical stressors do not undergo interpretation by the client, nor that psychological stressors do not have a physical impact or component. In fact, it can be easily argued that the body and mind, either liminally or subliminally, must interpret any stressor. However, physical stressors can be more useful when comparing clients' reactions to stress because of the greater physical component of the stressor and the relatively less important psychological component.

With pscyhological stressors, clients are being assessed on their psychological interpretation of the stressor *and* relaxation response to the stressor. Actually, this is what is being measured with all relaxation attempts during any stressor; and this fundamental idea must be kept in mind when interpreting any results.

Psychological stressors are varied, including verbal mathematics and spelling performance tests, photographs or slides with discomforting scenes, or requests to have the client mentally recall past stressful events. Obviously, each client responds to the psychological stressors based upon differences in past experiences, current individual and social expectations, and many other factors. This wide variability in psychological reaction to stressors makes basic interpretation of changes difficult.

Physical stressors can range from a cold pressor test (placing the hand in a cold water bath, or putting an ice cube on the forearm) to inducing mild pain with a clothespin on the earlobe. Other physical stressors include mild electrical stimuli to the skin, a gentle pinch or pinprick or a sudden loud noise (popping a balloon) that elicts a reflexive jump.

Physical stressors should never be continued to the point of severe pain. The client should be told beforehand that the stressor will be removed if he or she feels the stressor is becoming too much to bear. The client should also be informed that the physical stressor is being applied to help measure the client's ability to relax during a stressor—the physical stressor is not being used to test the client's ability to withstand pain or as a measure of the client's machismo.

When using a physical stressor, it is important to assess an individual's condition prior to the stressor being applied. Some individuals have medical conditions which could be exacerbated under the influence of a physical stressor (e.g., the cold pressor test leading to chest pain in a client with Printzmetal's Angina).[1]

SURVEY INSTRUMENTS

A wide variety of psychometric instruments for assessing personality, intelligence, mood states, cognitive styles, physical symptoms, values, etc. are presently in use. Some of these instruments assess an individual's readiness for various kinds of stress management interventions. Contrary to popular belief, there is not one test or assessment inventory which can measure an individual's stress level in a general manner, partly because of the wide variety of interpretations and connotations which surround the term. In the following sections, a number of inventories and assessment devices will be reviewed which may prove useful in assessing personality, situational, cognitive, and affective variables which might affect an individual's response to stress management interventions. Most of these instruments are easily administered, scored, and interpreted without the necessity for specialized training in psychometrics, or test theory and interpretation.

The descriptions of the different instruments are not complete and exhaustive, but are meant to provide a foundation for examining and selecting survey instruments for assessment procedures.

SYMPTOM CHECKLIST 90

The SCL 90 is a ninety-item inventory which requires the client to respond to a listing of common psychological and physical symptoms[2]. The client indicates, on a five point scale, the extent to which he or she is bothered by each symptom, ranging from "not at all" to "extremely." Scoring results in a profile of nine scales entitled Somatization, Obsessivity, Low Self-Esteem, Depression, Anxiety, Hostility, Phobic Anxiety, Paranoid Ideation, and Psychotocism. In addition, there are global indices of symptom severity, such as the Positive Symptom Distress Index and the Positive Symptom Total. The inventory is useful in identifying participants who may be experiencing intense psychological conflicts or significant physical symptoms which could significantly affect their response to relaxation training. Research studies have revealed that most individuals referred for biofeedback training have marked elevations on either the Depression or the Anxiety subscales. Individuals scoring high on the Low Self-Esteem, Hostility, Paranoid Ideation, and Psychotocism scales fare poorly in biofeedback training; it is recommended that these individuals participate in psychotherapy either before or during relaxation or biofeedback interventions. Finally, the symptom checklist serves as a quick assessment device for evaluating the type and breadth of physical symptoms experienced by the client; the interviewer may use the checklist as part of the intake interview process in order to assess the advisability of a medical referral.

Below are a couple of examples of inventory items on the SCL 90.

How much were you bothered by:

1.   having to do things very slowly to insure correctness?
2.   feeling shy or uneasy with the opposite sex?

STATE-TRAIT ANXIETY INVENTORY

The STAI is composed of two twenty-item inventories which assess the extent to which an individual is experiencing commonly accepted symptoms of anxiety. One inventory assesses state anxiety; that is, the transitory emotional state of a person at the time he or she is taking the test. The second inventory assesses trait anxiety, or the extent to which an individual *generally* experiences symptoms of anxiety[3]. Possible scores range from 20 to 80 points for both state and trait anxiety inventories. The inventory correlates fairly highly with other accepted anxiety measures, such as the Taylor Manifest Anxiety Scale and the IPAT Anxiety Scale. The State Anxiety subscale is useful for assessing periodic fluctuations in anxious mood and can be used to measure an individual's progress in learning to manage excessive stress and anxiety. The Trait Anxeity subscale is useful for identification of individuals who might experience difficulty in learning and applying stress management or relaxation techniques due to inordinately elevated levels of generalized or persistent anxiety. Those who obtain significantly elevated scores on this inventory (above the 85th percentile) may need special attention in learning stress management techniques. In addition, the inventory is short enough to be scanned quickly for positive responses to key items, which, if present, can be used to guide further inquiry. For example, if the individual responds positively to the item, "I feel that difficulties are piling up so that I cannot overcome them," the examiner might specifically ask what these difficulties are and, perhaps, make a counseling referral.

BECK DEPRESSION INVENTORY

Depression is one of the most common psychological disabilities affecting humankind. Commonly reported symptoms include pervasive feelings of sadness and guilt, a sense of hopelessness about the future, difficulties with sleeping behavior, appetite changes, feelings of worthlessness and helplessness, inability to concentrate, and a lack of energy. Clinical depression, as contrasted with more normal blue mood states, persists at least several weeks at a time, and may last several years for many individuals. Even though there is disagreement as to the best treatment for depression, most clinicians believe some combination of drug therapy and intensive, short-term psychotherapy or counseling offers the best solution for assisting depressed individuals to overcome their symptoms. Moderate or severe symptoms can substantially interfere with an individual's ability to gain from relaxation or biofeedback training programs. Those psychological traits which influence success in such programs are precisely the ones which are likely to be minimal or absent in depression—self-confidence, expectations of success, motivation, enthusiasm, and self-responsibility.

The Beck Depression Inventory can be a useful tool in identifying participants in relaxation programs who are suffering from depressive symptoms[4]. The inventory is short (only twenty-one items) and easy to administer, score, and interpret. The authors of the test suggest that overall scores of 15 or more indicate that depressive symptoms are substantial and appropriate psychological or medical referral is indicated. As in the tests surveyed earlier, the Beck Depression Inventory can also be scanned for critical responses to individual items. If necessary, the client can be questioned to provide additional details so that appropriate interpretations and interventions can be made. For example, if the client responds "Yes" to the item, "I feel I am a complete failure as a person," it is likely that he or she will perceive their inability to make substantial gains from a relaxation training program as another indication that their self-concept of a failure is true. The item, "I have no appetite at all anymore," may indicate that a significant clinical depression exists that quite likely can be helped by the appropriate use of antidepressant medication. Only when these clinical symptoms are under control can the individual really be expected to make significant gains in a stress management program.

SOCIAL READJUSTMENT RATING SCALE

Around the turn of the century, Adolf Meyer, professor of psychiatry at Johns Hopkins University, realized that his patients tended to get sick around the time when clusters of major events or changes occurred in their lives. Building upon these observations, Thomas Holmes developed a rating scale which listed many of the changes individuals typically experience during their lives. Marriage was arbitrarily assigned a value of fifty points, and clients then rated other change items as to how much more or less each required in adjustment when compared to marriage. For example, the scale indicates that the death of a spouse requires twice as much adjustment as getting married, or that it requires four times as much adjustment as a change in living conditions. Follow-up research conducted by Holmes indicated that the higher an individual's total score, the more likely the individual will report changes in health or well-being. For example, in one study, Rahe discovered that 30% of the enlisted men with the highest life-change scores developed nearly 90% more of the initial illnesses during the first month of their tour of duty than the 30%

with the lowest life-change scores.

The authors of the test indicate that if an individual scores between 150 and 300 points, the chances of entering the hospital rise to a 50-50 chance. If the score is more than 300 points, the chance of entering the hospital for some illness rises to 90%.[5]

The inventory is easily scored and interpreted by the client and can serve as a powerful training tool in its own right: clients can begin to develop an awareness of what the stressors are in their lives. The inventory is somewhat limited in that it does not measure the adaptive potential of the individual in question (i.e., some individuals appear to take changes in lifestyle with very little apparent stress-related symptoms), nor is the inventory able to assess how the individual interprets the changes which have occurred (i.e., one individual may be relieved to hear that one job opportunity is lost, while another individual may see the lost job opportunity as a more serious loss or threat). Still, the inventory provides a useful diagnostic and training tool for those teaching stress management.

JENKINS ACTIVITY SURVEY

In 1974, Friedman and Rosenman identified "Type A Behavior" as a personality trait characterized by a chronic, aggressive, incessant struggle to acheive more and more in less and less time.[6] The pattern also includes excessive time urgency, competitive striving, hostility, and a low sense of security. A strong association between Type A behavior and coronary heart disease was demonstrated initially in a major study involving 3,145 men[7,8] that determined that the annual rate of coronary heart disease was 13.2 cases per 1000 men with Type A Behavior, as contrasted with 5.9 cases for 1000 men with Type B Behavior (i.e., those without the Type A Behavior). A variety of methods have been used to identify the Type A personality. The Jenkins Activity Survey is, perhaps, the one most often used.

This survey is a self-administered, machine- or hand-scored

questionnaire which measures four factors: speed and impatience, job involvement, hard driving and competitiveness, plus an overall Type A score. It consists of forty-four multiple-choice questions. About half of the items in the survey are used as distractor items to mask the true behaviors being analyzed. Scores can range from 0 to 21, with a very low score (0 - 5) indicating a strong Type B behavior, a low score (6 - 10) indicating a weak Type B behavior, a medium high score (11 - 15) indicating a weak Type A behavior, and a high score (16 - 21) indicating a strong Type A behavior.

There is an alternate form (Form T) that was developed for use with college and university student populations. Both the adult and the student forms use 21 items to discriminate coronary prone behaviors, and there is little difference between the two forms. The Jenkins Activity Survey has a high degree of internal consistency[9] and high concurrent and construct validity.[10,11]

Below are examples of questions in the Jenkins Activity Survey (Form T):

A. When you are under pressure or stress, do you usually:
  1. Do something about it immediately.
  2. Plan carefully before taking any action.

B. How was your "temper" when you were younger?
  1. Fiery and hard to control.
  2. Strong, but controllable.
  3. No problem.
  4. I almost never got angry.

The Jenkins Activity Survey test results can provide hard data for the client—it is hard to argue with a test result which indicates that one is in the upper 10% of the population in terms of Type A behavior! Such results might provide motivation for the individual to participate in a stress-management program, although little research has been done to assess the motivational impact of such data on an individual's interest in learning effective stress management behaviors.

For the facilitator, such test results can be used to gain data regarding the likely response of workshop participants to the content of the course. For example, individuals with significantly elevated scores on this test can be expected to be impatient with what they perceive as slow progress in noticing benefits of stress management practices. These individuals will likely become bored and restless when listening to long relaxation instructions or, worse, may be at risk of prematurely terminating a relaxation training course if they do not experience instant, perfect results with the training.

TAYLOR MANIFEST ANXIETY SCALE

The Taylor Manifest Anxiety Scale is a fifty question survey of client perceptions about physiological and psychological reactions to life and stressful events. The test is in a True-False format and can be taken within ten minutes. Below are two sample questions:

A. I have periods of such great restlessness that I cannot sit long in a chair.
B. I sweat very easily, even on cool days.

Scores can range from 0 to 50, with a low score indicating a low level of perceived physical stress symptoms and a high score indicating an excessive level of perceived physical stress symptoms. It is important to remember that some individuals are more sensitive to physical symptoms and body cues than others, so that a high score on the Taylor Manifest Anxiety scale may reflect sensitivity to body cues more than an increase in actual physical symptoms of stress. Excessive stress symptom scores (35 points or greater) point to the fact that the client believes he or she is exhibiting a high number of physical symptoms of stress. The client, with the facilitator's assistance, should intervene to reduce these symptoms. The average score for the Taylor Manifest

Anxiety Scale is 19 points, with the score of 7 points marking the lower 20th percentile, and the score of 31 points marking the upper 20th percentile.

GENERAL WELL-BEING SCHEDULE

The General Well-Being Schedule was developed by Dr. Harold Dupuy for the National Health and Nutrition Examination Surveys conducted by the National Center for Health Statistics. The self-administered instrument was designed to "assess selected aspects of self-representations of subjective well-being and distress."[12] The schedule is composed of 25 questions that use a multiple choice or rating scale format. When completed, clients are scored for a Total Well-Being Score and six Adjustment Factor subscales: Freedom from health concern; Energy level; Satisfying, interesting life; Cheerful versus depressed mood; Relaxed versus tense-anxious; and Emotional-behavioral control.

The General Well-Being Schedule has undergone extensive testing and has been shown to be highly reliable and valid. It appears that the General Well-Being Schedule zeros in on the psychological states of depression and anxiety as its major measures for lack of well-being.

Clients can score from 0 to 110 points for the Total Well-Being Score, with a score of 0 to 55 indicating clinically significant distress, a score of 56 to 70 signifying problem-indicative stress, and a score from 71 to 110 signifying positive well-being. The mean for the Total Well-Being Score was 80.3 points for the 6,931 subjects in the Health and Nutrition Examination Survey conducted between 1971 and 1975. The mean score for the 195 students in the validational study was 72.4 points.[13]

Below is a sample of questions from the General Well Being Schedule.

1. Have you been under or felt you were under any strain, stress, or pressure? *(during the past month)*
    1. Yes — almost more than I could bear or stand
    2. Yes — quite a bit of pressure
    3. Yes — some - more than usual
    4. Yes — some - about usual
    5. Yes — a little
    6. Not at all

2. Has your daily life been full of things that were interesting to you? *(during the past month)*
    1. All of the time
    2. Most of the time
    3. A good bit of the time
    4. Some of the time
    5. A little of the time
    6. None of the time

AN EVALUATION HANDBOOK FOR HEALTH EDUCATION PROGRAMS IN STRESS MANAGEMENT

In an effort to provide leadership and guidance for evaluation efforts in the field of health education, The Center for Health Promotion and Education at the Centers for Disease Control has developed a series of evaluation handbooks. One book in this series deals specifically with outcomes associated with stress management activities among the adult, adolescent, and elementary school children populations. In essence, specialists within the fields of stress management and evaluation studies combined energies to identify and/or construct program evaluation goals that would be most beneficial in measuring the impacts of stress management activities, courses, or programs. The three major outcomes that the experts identified were: (1) using stress management techniques, (2) avoiding life stress, and (3) life satisfaction. Program outcome statements were developed for the knowledge, affective, skill, and behavioral realms, reaching across all age levels. Below is a sample of a few program outcome statements found in the evaluation handbook:

Knowledge Outcomes

Individuals can accurately recall information about the nature of stress responses. This information includes the nature of common external stressors, the basic physiology of stress, the potential effects of stress on individuals, and the stress-related aspects of diet.

Affective Outcomes

Individuals believe that they can manage the stress associated with various aspects of their daily lives, including physical stress, symbolic stress, overload, frustration, and deprivation.

Skill Outcomes

Individuals can choose courses of action that are appropriate responses to stress.

Behavioral Outcomes

Individuals use a variety of techniques that can help them manage their stress.

The above program outcome statements, and ones like them, were then used to identify current instruments that would be potential assessment instruments. The General Well-Being Schedule, the Personal Feelings Inventory, and the National Institute on Drug Abuse Life Satisfaction Questionnaire are three such instruments. New instruments were developed if no existing instrument could be found to match with the generated program outcome statements.

This manual on stress management program evaluation presents already established, validated instruments, and introduces many new, yet-to-be-validated instruments. Both norm-referenced and criterion-referenced tests are presented, with a heavy emphasis towards criterion-reference evaluation in the newly developed tests. In total, thirty-two new measures and nine existing measures are presented in the manual. Most of the new instruments are short (approximately twenty questions or less), and test specifications are provided for each instrument in the handbook.

The Evaluation Handbook for Health Education Programs in Stress Management has initial chapters that consider such important topics as: conducting evaluation studies, selecting appropriate measures, sampling considerations for data collection, linking measurement and program design, data analysis, and using the handbook's measures correctly. Although studies demonstrating the validity and reliability of the handbook's measures will need to be performed, the handbook provides valuable information to aid in assessing stress management training efforts.[14]

•••••••• INSTRUCTIONAL POINTERS ••••••••

1.   *Wide varieties of surveys, inventories, and tests are available to the stress management facilitator, any of which are easy to administer, score, and interpret. As a rule, the facilitator should consider the specific population enrolled in the workshop or program and what specific outcomes or learning opportunities are desired for the participants, before selecting any tests to be used for assessment or educational purposes.*

2.   *Be careful not to overload clients with stress management assessments: they may become irritated or overwhelmed if asked to complete too many prior to beginning a training program. Remember that the assessment tools can be used very effectively by spacing them throughout the workshop and relating them to the specific content of the workshop. The Jenkins Activity Survey, Social Readjustment Scale, General Well-Being Schedule, Taylor Manifest Anxiety Survey, and instruments from the Evaluation Handbook in Stress Management may be more appropriately used during the workshop to illustrate important points related to stress management. Clinical assessments with biofeedback instruments can help point out important concepts and physiological changes within clients.*

3.   *Instruments can be used to assess the readiness of individuals coming to a stress management training program, to educate participants about their own stress-related personality factors, and to determine the effectiveness of the stress management training program. The Symptom Checklist 90, Beck Depression Inventory, and State-Trait Anxiety Inventory may be very useful as initial assessment or screening tools before the training process begins so that appropriate* counseling interventions may be made on those who need more psychotherapeutic assistance than a stress management training program may provide. Obviously, some assessment instruments may be useful in both circumstances.

4. The Taylor Manifest Anxiety Scale, State-Trait Anxiety Inventory, Beck Depression Inventory, Symptom Checklist 90, General Well-Being Schedule, and some assessment instruments from the Evaluation handbook in Stress Management can be used to provide preintervention and postintervention comparisons for assessing changes in symptoms, moods, stress level, etc. This can provide objective feedback to the client about the progress he or she has made, and to the facilitator about the impact of his or her intervention.

CHAPTER 17

ENHANCING BEHAVIOR CHANGE IN STRESS MANAGEMENT CLIENTS

LEVELS OF INTERVENTION FOR STRESS MANAGEMENT

In Chapter 14, a model for understanding biofeedback interventions depicted a four-stage process by which individuals perceive events, interpret them, experience physiological reactions based on the interpretation, which then results in behavioral outcomes in an effort to cope with the events. This four-stage model is a convenient tool for analyzing which level (event, interpretation, physiological reaction, behavioral outcome) is the most suitable for interventions in stress management. This section presents a variety of interventions available for use at all four levels and provides several examples of how to make effective interventions at each level.

A common fault of health care practitioners is the tendency to consider one's own area of expertise and training as the primary mode and level of intervention for every individual who seeks help. While this narrow focus for managing most types of human problems is unavoidable, many times other potential spheres of intervention which play crucial roles in the particular problem presented to us by our clients are ignored. The model in Figure 17-1 helps us conceptualize the various levels of intervention with clients who seek help in stress management. A crucial point to keep in mind is that failure to address levels other than one's favorite level may increase the likelihood that intervention will not have the potential impact desired.

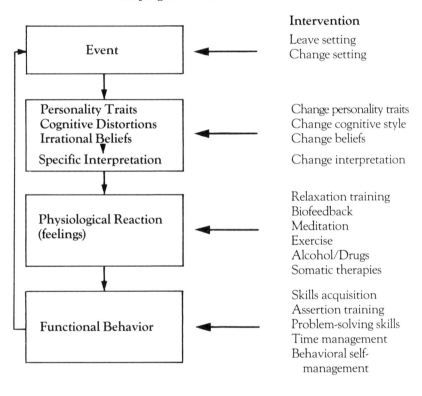

Figure 17 - 1

Helping: Levels of Intervention

	Intervention
Event	Leave setting Change setting
Personality Traits **Cognitive Distortions** **Irrational Beliefs** **Specific Interpretation**	Change personality traits Change cognitive style Change beliefs Change interpretation
Physiological Reaction **(feelings)**	Relaxation training Biofeedback Meditation Exercise Alcohol/Drugs Somatic therapies
Functional Behavior	Skills acquisition Assertion training Problem-solving skills Time management Behavioral self- management

Case 1: Tom

Tom is a college sophomore taking a full load of courses in his desire to gain admission into medical school. He comes into a stress management course with the desire to learn to relax and experience less anxiety related to his studies. The initial interview reveals that Tom experiences considerable feelings of anxiety for several days preceding a major exam in his physics and chemistry classes. Tom admits that this test anxiety substantially interferes with his performance on the test. The question he asks is, "How can this stress management class help me make better grades on my tests?"

Let us consider interventions at all four levels. First, intervention at the Event Level might lead us to consider advising Tom to reduce his load of difficult courses this semester, and thus reduce the likelihood he will be confronted with difficult tests as often as he is. This level of intervention may also mean that Tom has to consider other vocations (provided he is unable to continue to perform acceptably in the pre-medical school program). Interventions at this level alone can be unacceptable.

The second level of intervention, attempting to help Tom change his attitude or cognitive interpretations of taking tests, might prove to be a more productive approach. For example, further discussion with Tom might reveal that he approaches tests in an unrealistic manner. He might be engaging in the following self-talk: "I had better do well on this test—my whole future depends on the outcome," or "I can't stand taking tests. I know I will do poorly. Everyone else will do better than I will." Knowing that Tom keeps himself in a high state of arousal by continually feeding himself these extreme and unrealistic remarks might lead us to suggest to Tom that he repeat the following statements to himself prior to taking a test: "I am as prepared as I can be, I will just go in and do my best. This test is not a measure of my self-worth or even my intelligence; it is merely an indication of how well I am able to guess what this teacher thinks is important to know about this course. If I fail it, it will be a disappointment, but it is not the end of the world...." Such a cognitive intervention might reduce the extreme physiological arousal Tom experiences upon taking tests.

Interventions at the third level, modifying physiological reactions or affective responses, include what we are most likely better trained to do: relaxation training, biofeedback therapy, and the like. The typical lay person is also, interestingly, most likely to consider intervening at this level by taking pain killers or tranquilizers, or by consuming cigarettes, food, or alcohol. Using Tom's situation as an example once again, we can teach some general relaxation skills and also teach him to practice some brief relaxation maneuvers just prior to and during the test itself. (See Chapter 15 for more detail.)

Finally, at the fourth level of intervention where behavioral alterations are made, we can teach Tom more effective study and test-taking techniques, such as making outlines of text readings, using the SQ3R method of reading materials, listing those major points that the course instructor considered important, and, when taking the test itself, rereading the test instructions, pacing the test to the allotted time, dealing with easier questions first, etc.

By addressing all four levels, we are in a much better position to assist Tom in overcoming the debilitating symptoms of stress which originally brought him to the stress management workshop. It is important to realize that it is difficult to be equipped to intervene on all four levels ourselves. Knowledge of useful referral resources outside our own specialized level of intervention is important to consider and to have ready to use. For instance, Tom can be referred to the study skills services on his college campus for help in learning effective test-taking. Or, he can be referred to the counseling center for help in overcoming unproductive or self-defeating attitudes towards academic performance.

Case 2: Susan

Susan enrolled in a stress management workshop and complained of anxiety, insomnia, a compulsive drive to accomplish tasks perfectly, feelings of alienation from others, a chronic inability to slow down, and a conviction that she was getting less and less done with more and more time being wasted.

Susan presents a picture of the Type A personality pattern so aptly described by Friedman and Rosenman.[1] These authors characterize the Type A pattern as one where the individual fears loss of mastery and control of a wide range of situations and activities in his or her life. Typically, this individual expresses constant impatience with the pace of activities and conversations, and always attempts to be on top of every situation. There is an underlying sense of repressed hostility which characterizes their interpersonal encounters, and it has been found that such personality types have a greater than average chance of developing cardiovascular disease later in life. What is the best intervention for this individual? By focusing solely on relaxation training, meditation, or biofeedback training, we stand the chance of losing this client after a few meetings. Since this type of person perceives relaxing as a waste of time or a boring event, Susan may quickly become frustrated and leave the training feeling more anxious than when she began the treatment!

Interventions at the event level might involve teaching Susan how to avoid certain stressful situations or encounters or, ultimately, to consider changing careers to an area which is less stressful. It should be noted, however, that removing oneself from a stressful environment is usually perceived by the Type A individual as a sign of failure and, therefore, is not as likely to occur.

Interventions on the cognitive, or interpretive, level might involve helping Susan change the meaning attributed to situations in her life. Teaching such responses as, "There is no need to overreact to this stress," or "I'll win this threatening encounter by acting cool," or "Why involve my body in this stressful situation?" may help Susan respond less stressfully to life conditions.

Attitudes towards relaxation training might be altered by saying "Relaxation training will assist the client in becoming more productive and effective at work," or "I'm sure you can learn this brief relaxation skill - although it might be somewhat of a challenge to you to do so!" Such statements work with the Type A personality in helping them take on the challenge of learning to relax.

Finally, interventions at the level of behavioral outcomes might include assertiveness training to teach Susan skills in saying "No" to those who want her to take on more projects, activities, or responsibilities. Communication skills may aid her in learning how to communicate more empathically with her colleagues. Time management instruction may assist her in becoming more efficient in getting the most important things done and leaving the less important projects out of her life.

Once again, it is not the single level intervention that would be most effective but a comprehensive approach to stress management intervention that works best.

As a final observation, a useful training technique is to have the client assess his or her present level of functioning, considering all four levels of intervention in Table 17-1. For example, the typical harried housewife might: (1) list all the events or settings which she finds herself in that cause her stress; (2) analyze what sorts of attitudes, cognitive interpretations, beliefs, etc., that contribute to her physical reactions to stress; (3) be guided in an exploration of how her body physically responds to the stressful events; (4) assess what skills she needs to cope more effectively with the stressors in her life. Used this way, the chart in Figure 17-1 is an assessment tool to more efficiently guide the stress management interventions which must be made.

A MODEL OF BEHAVIOR APPROPRIATE
TO STRESS MANAGEMENT TRAINING

Operant learning theory states that behavior is a function of consequences. According to this theory, all human behavior is maintained, strengthened, or weakened depending on whether such behavior is followed by positive or negative reinforcement. As such, the key to changing any behavior lies in changing the environmental contingencies (patterns of reinforcement) which immediately follow the behavior. Applied to stress management, this concept means that our response to stressful events in our lives can be altered by examining and changing the patterns of positive and negative reinforcements which follow the behavior in question.

For example, many executives in positions of responsibility have been reinforced to behave in ways which may prove ultimately harmful to their health. Working long hours, displaying verbal and behavioral aggressiveness, making work tasks a number one priority, and hiding feelings are usually considered desirable behaviors which are reinforced by promotions, increases in salary, prestige, and verbal praise by superiors. As such, the behavior is maintained. At the same time, there are negative reinforcers which compete with the overt positive reinforcers, such as increasing feelings of irritability, anxiety, and verbal complaints from friends and family that they are burning the candle at both ends. According to learning theory, the relative potency of these various overt and covert reinforcers determines just how much such Type A behaviors persist. Behavioral interventions might include quitting the job (i.e., removing the individual from the job-related reinforcers), changing the reward structure of the corporate world, increasing the potency of the reinforcements towards more healthy behaviors, or changing the meaning of the rewards to the individual.

To the extent that the external reward systems cannot be easily altered (i.e., it is unlikely that the business world will soon begin to reward taking time for oneself), it is desirable to assist the individual in creating different reward structures and systems for more healthful behaviors, parallel to the reward system in which he or she is currently participating. For example, learning theory indicates that in order to maintain a regular, consistent relaxation practice schedule, the client must experience reward as a result of engaging in the training. Such rewards might include (1) keeping a chart of relaxation practice time and giving oneself a rewarding experience or prize when a certain criterion is met, (2) giving oneself positive self-talk as a result of successfully completing a practice session, or (3) reminding one's spouse to verbally reward the relaxation practice. The ultimate goal of relaxation training is to have the participant experience potent *internal* rewards, as a result of the relaxation training process itself, so that the artificially-created environmental reward structures can be phased out.

During the last several years, there has been increasing acceptance of the role cognitive variables have in affecting behavior. It is not enough that the individual simply respond passively to external positive and negative reinforcements. The individual's own interpretation of the impact of various rewards is a crucial variable in designing more effective reward systems for enhancing stress management. For example, if the Type A executive views relaxing as being lazy or unproductive, he or she will be less likely to incorporate this skill in everyday life. On the other hand, if this individual interprets relaxation training as actually increasing their work efficiency in the long run, then this person will be more likely to persist with the training sessions.

Self-talk is the term given to how we interpret and respond to the meanings we attach to the stress management interventions. Self-talk operates on two different levels. First, instead of permitting ourselves to react automatically to the stressful events which occur in our lives, we can actively talk to ourselves about these events in a manner which might reduce the perceived threat in such events. For example, we can say to ourselves, "Stay calm, there is no need for an argument," or "Getting upset won't help either of us," or "He would probably like to see me get angry, so I'm going to disappoint him," and hence have direct control over how we physically respond to threatening encounters. Unless we actively and consciously talk to ourselves in this fashion, we will not overcome the more negative, threat-inducing responses which automatically occur in such situations. A second aspect of how self-talk can be useful relates to positive reinforcement. After we have successfully handled a stressful encounter or event, we can deliver covert reinforcement to ourselves by saying, "It worked! I'm getting better at this all the time," or "Congratulations, you handled that encounter very well. You deserve a pat on the back." Such covert, cognitive reinforcements can be potent shapers of more effective stress-management behaviors. The chart in Figure 17-2 depicts the various types of reinforcement that can help alter one's habitual response to stress. We can create reinforcements which are either positive or negative, and we can either use or remove them if they already exist. The chart depicts the effect on the behavior in question. For example, if we present a pleasurable experience (Box 1) following a certain behavior, the frequency of that behavior will likely increase. On the other hand, if we remove a pleasurable experience, it is likely that the behavior will decrease (Box 3).

In applying reinforcement theory to stress management, Box 1 might be illustrated by rewarding yourself with some desired purchase provided you listen to a relaxation tape every day during one week. Box 2 can be illustrated by administering some punishment to yourself if you do not adhere to a decision to practice a stress management skill. For example, you might have created an agreement with your biofeedback facilitator that if you do not maintain weekly charts of your relaxation training at home, you will have to pay a predetermined fine. An example of

Box 3 could be foregoing a night out with your bowling partners if you neglected to engage in your prescribed exercise activity. And, finally, Box 4 might be illustrated by agreeing that your spouse will hide your mail and not let you read it until you have listened to your relaxation tape. It should be noted that there are endless variations for creating effective reinforcement strategies to assist an individual's adherence to any component of a stress management program. Also, one should not rely heavily on Boxes 2 and 3 because these types of reinforcements tend to increase stress and anxiety (punishment is not the best reinforcer).

Figure 17 - 2

Classification of Reinforcement

	Pleasurable Experience	Aversive Experience
Present	Positive reinforcement Behavior increases	Negative reinforcement Behavior decreases
Remove	Negative reinforcement Behavior decreases	Positive reinforcement Behavior increases

Most successful interventions utilize strategies exemplified by Boxes 1 and 4. Finally, keep in mind that these artificial reinforcement procedures are temporary and can be phased out as the natural reinforcing consequences of good stress management practices begin to occur. As you begin to notice changes in how you feel, which are rewarding in their own right, there will be less of a need to apply external reinforcement strategies in an effort to change behavior. For further information and strategies using behavioral interventions, the reader is advised to consult Burns,[2] Mahoney and Thoreson,[3] and Watson and Tharp.[4]

COGNITIVE VARIABLES INFLUENCING STRESS MANAGEMENT

As noted in the previous section, cognitive and attitudinal variables play a critical role in our reactions to stressful events. In addition, cognitive variables determine our attitude towards, and our reaction to, any interventions made in our response to stress. This section considers the role of cognitive distortions and irrational beliefs as significant contributors to unnecessarily stressful reactions to events.

COGNITIVE DISTORTIONS

Table 17-1 lists five important types of cognitive distortions which affect how we interpret and respond to stressful events. The more frequently these distortions are used and believed, the greater the stressful reactions will be.

The first distortion, All-or-Nothing Thinking, is commonly observed in individuals who portray the Type A pattern described earlier. All-or-Nothing thinking characterizes their statements:

"I had better get all A's in this class or else I'll give up."
"If I don't lose 20 pounds by the end of the month, I'm a failure and I will give up this crummy diet."

"If I am not able to relax myself completely during this relaxation session, it means I will never learn this stuff."
"I had better get over thse headaches for good—if they come back, relaxation training is useless."

Table 17 - 1

Cognitive Distortions

1. *All-or-Nothing Thinking:* You see things in black-and-white categories. If your performance falls short of perfect, you see yourself as a total failure.
2. *Overgeneralization:* You see a single negative event as a never-ending pattern of defeat.
3. *Catastrophizing (Magnification):* You exaggerate the importance of things (such as your negative traits or someone else's achievement), or you discredit your own desirable qualities and accomplishments.
4. *Personalization:* You see yourself as the cause of some negative external event that in fact you were not primarily responsible for.
5. *Labeling:* This is an extreme form of overgeneralization. Instead of describing your error in behavioral terms, you attach a negative label to yourself: "I'm a loser."

From D. Burns, *Feeling Good: The New Mood Therapy*
(New York: Signet, 1980).

When clients make such remarks, it is important to dispute them by restating them in a less distorted fashion. For example, a less distorted response to each of the above statements might be:

"I may or may not get all A's in this class. In any case, it is unrealistic to think that I would be a failure simply because I did not live up to this expectation."

"I will lose whatever weight my body decides to lose - why should it comply with some arbitrary figure my mind decides upon? I will take just one day at a time."

"It may take some time to learn to relax. Just because I don't relax my muscles this session does not mean I am a failure. Success in any endeavor takes practice and patience."

"If I can simply reduce the frequency or the severity of these headaches, I will consider this stress management program a success."

It is easy to see that this second set of statements is more reasonable, realistic, and appropriate than the first set.

The second cognitive distortion, Overgeneralization, is a variation of the All-or-Nothing Thinking distortion. Overgeneralization involves concluding that a single negative event signifies a never-ending pattern of defeat. For example, if during relaxation training, a client becomes aware of increased muscle pains in his shoulders, he may wrongfully conclude that, "I obviously am not ever going to learn relaxation training!" Such individuals view the world through grey-colored glasses - positive signs of change or improvement are ignored and a single sign of some negative event is seen as all-encompassing. Individuals who overgeneralize are prone to give up at the first signs of experiencing a failure. The person who undertakes an exercise program may conclude that it is fruitless to continue exercising simply because she missed one day last week. This type of cognitive distortion needs to be confronted head on. You might say to them, "Just because you suffered one set back or experienced this one negative event does not necessarily mean that you are doomed to failure—unless, of course, you choose to think that way in order to have a ready excuse for not continuing with the program."

A third example of a cognitive distortion is called Catastrophizing. Catastrophizing is magnifying the likelihood of some terrible potential event and dwelling on the certainty of its occurrence until all present experience is ignored. This cognitive distortion is reflected in statements such as, "I know I will not succeed in this relaxation class. Look how relaxed everyone else is. I know I will fail." Needless to say, such thinking likely will hasten the arrival of the very prediction that is feared; a self-fulfilling prophecy is created which confirms the original prediction. Another side of this type of thinking lies in the statement, "I'm having an irregular heart beat. I know beyond a shadow of a doubt that this means that I will have a heart attack next." This catastrophic predicting creates more anxiety, which in turn causes increased physiological stress to occur and, in this case, makes the likelihood of cardiac irregularities rise.

The fourth cognitive distortion often found in clients is called Personalization. It is defined as taking excessive responsibility for some event. For example, a mother who assumes the blame for the negative behaviors of one of her children might state, "I'm a failure as a mother because Johnny was sent home from school." This type of reaction is guaranteed to create unnecessary stress and anxiety which no relaxation program alone can successfully alter. Once you can teach the client that she has only partial responsibility for other people's misfortunes (even her own children), then she can be helped to reduce the frequency of her stress reactions as she encounters such behaviors in others. "Take responsibility for your own behavior, and let others take responsibility for theirs" is one response to this type of thinking. Personalization is also noted in the attitudes of certain health care professionals who have experienced some failures in their treatment of patients or clients. They conclude that they have been ineffective or, worse, incompetent and, therefore, should begin to look for other types of work. This is erroneous thinking which is responsible, perhaps, for the degree of burnout seen in many areas of the helping professions. A more appropriate attitude might be, "I will do what I can for these clients, but the rest is up to them. I cannot be totally responsible for all their successes, nor can I be responsible for all their failures."

The final cognitive distortion is called Labeling. This distortion has already been portrayed in some of the examples above: labeling oneself a failure because of a perceived inability to reach a goal; or labeling oneself as a patient, with the connotations of being helpless to manage one's own health or always being affected by certain symptoms. While labeling may have a useful role in assisting someone to diagnose his or her situation (i.e., discovering that I am a Type A personality), it loses its effectiveness when it interferes with change. Coupled with all-or-nothing thinking, labeling can be especially pernicious. For example, "If I am a Type A personality, then the goal of this relaxation program must be to make me into a Type B personality, which would be terrible!" A better approach might be to say, "You exhibit some of the characteristics of the Type A pattern, and we will help you bring some of the more deleterious effects of this pattern under control, making you happier and even more productive. But we are not going to make you into a Type B personality, even if that were possible (because it probably is not)."

It is important to remember that everyone probably engages in these kinds of illogical reasoning. Many therapists believe that those people who think in distorted fashions about the events in their lives will experience more anxiety, tension, confusion, and unhappiness. Making relaxation clients aware of the presence of this type of thinking will give them another tool for correcting their maladaptive responses to stress.

There are several more varieties of cognitive distortions which have not been discussed. For further analysis and study refer to the book, *Feeling Good*, by David Burns.[5] You might want to recommend this book to clients if you suspect that they are unnecessarily increasing the stress they experience through excessive cognitive distortions.

IRRATIONAL BELIEFS

Another type of cognitive misbehavior is Irrational Beliefs or expectations on the part of clients who seek help in managing stress. Albert Ellis is the individual most closely associated with the idea that irrational or inappropriate beliefs and expectations are responsible for much of the unnecessary misery people cause themselves.[6] While cognitive distortions are *patterns* of thinking which are inappropriate or distorted, irrational beliefs refer to the actual *beliefs and attitudes* people have regarding how the world really is. Table 17-2 lists several of the irrational beliefs often expressed by individuals.

Table 17 - 2

Irrational Beliefs

1. It is a dire necessity to be loved and approved by virtually every significant other person in his or her community.
2. One should be thoroughly competent, adequate, and achieving in all possible respects if one is to consider oneself worthwhile.
3. It is awful and catastrophic when things are not the way one would very much like them to be.
4. Human unhappiness is externally caused and people have little or no ability to control their sorrows and disturbances.
5. One's past history is an all-important determiner of one's present behavior and because something once strongly affected one's life, it should indefinitely have a similar effect.
6. There is invariably a right, precise, and perfect solution to human problems and it is catastrophic if this perfect solution is not found.

From A. Ellis & R. Harper, *A New Guide to Rational Living*
(Hollywood, CA: Wilshire Book Co., 1979).

The first irrational belief is most commonly expressed by women in our culture, and it makes it difficult for many women to assertively set limits to the demands placed upon them by family, friends, and job associates. Individuals who approve of this belief find it difficult to say no to unreasonable requests from others and, as a result, find themselves overwhelmed with the number of projects, tasks, responsibilities, and duties. A more appropriate belief might be stated, "It is indeed nice to be loved and approved by many people, but it is eminently unrealistic to expect that you can be all things to all people. If you do, you are simply creating a hopeless existence for yourself and no amount of exercise, relaxation training, good nutrition, or biofeedback training will make much difference."

The second irrational belief is one which appears to be firmly held by the Type A personality. This individual feels that any effort short of 100% is to be ridiculed. "Do your best" is his motto, and it extends to all areas of activity. Any falling short of his goals is not to be tolerated. Indeed, if the goals are not met, such an individual is likely to jump to the opposite extreme and give up. This attitude also extends to the stress management interventions they are asked to make. For example, relaxation facilitators know there are some people who try too hard to relax and are afraid of not acheiving the best possible results in the shortest period of time. These individuals are likely to drop out of the program if this type of irrational belief is not confronted early and replaced with a more reasonable set of expectations, such as, "It is *not* possible to be totally adequate, competent, and achieving all the time, or even half of the time. *I* will decide when high personal expectations have the best likelihood of providing me with the rewards I seek. I will allow myself to join the rest of the human race and behave in an average manner."

The third belief is also often discovered in highly striving, competitive individuals who need to have total control over every setting or experience in which they find themselves. Such people fear giving up control and, as such, find themselves experiencing anxiety over any situation which threatens loss of control. They also have great difficulty learning relaxation and destressing skills which require a more trusting attitude of letting go in order to experience the full effects of relaxation. They will likely report they are relaxed when physiological indicators show the opposite. Have these individuals proceed slowly and gain experience with the new, unusual feeling of losing control. They need to experience the pleasure of going with the flow and to accept that not all things will turn out the way they want. It might be beneficial for them to contemplate on a more realistic statement of this belief, "While it is unpleasant when things do not go the way we want, it certainly is not awful or catastrophic. I can be much happier if I allow myself to bend with the surprises, interruptions, confusions, and hangups that occur during my day, rather than fight something that may be out of my control."

The fourth belief has both a positive and a negative side. While it is important to realize that indeed some events are outside of our control (Belief 3), it is false to assume that our *interpretations and reactions* to these events are equally uncontrollable. It is important to realize that much of human unhappiness is influenced by the way people *interpret* events in their lives. (Indeed, this thought is the thesis of this whole section.) When it is impossible to affect the events themselves, it is always possible to change the way we perceive or view those events. As such, a better expression of this belief might be, " While much of human unhappiness is indeed externally caused, I do have the ability (unless I choose to give it up) to control how I react to events in my life and, to that extent, I do have the ability to control how mad, sad, afraid, anxious, or happy I shall feel at any given moment."

The fifth belief once again illustrates how individuals are all too ready to give up control over how they live their lives and how they respond to events which occur. These individuals will say, "I grew up in a very unhappy home life and because of that I have no hope of ever changing my level of success or happiness in the future." Clients who carry this conviction around will be hard to train in relaxation and stress management skills because they firmly believe that their symptoms of stress are indeed outside their control and are caused by events which occurred earlier in their lives (e.g., once a Type A, always a Type A). Actually, this belief provides many people with the excuse not to do anything about their miserable existence and may even be a comforting thought to some people who are frightened of the opportunity to make significant changes in how they respond to stressful events. The belief should be disputed by posing an alternative, "While indeed your history is an important determinant of your present state, it is certainly not the most important influence. You can always choose to affirm this irrational belief whenever you are scared about making important changes in your life and in the way you handle stress."

Finally, the sixth belief appears to be another expression of the All-or-Nothing cognitive distortion discussed earlier. Clients who express this attitude will almost certainly disappoint themselves and whoever they are working with in stress management programs. This attitude can be heard in the statement, "I would really like to learn relaxation skills so that I can get rid of all my back pain, increase my rewards at my job, make my children respect me, and gain more attention and love from my spouse. If this is not possible, then refer me to someone else." A better approach is to say to your clients, "This relaxation program will not cure you of anything. It probably will not dramatically change your life, nor is it the key to instant happiness. However, if you decide to seriously practice the strategies I am about to teach you, you will notice certain changes occurring in the way you approach stressful events in your life and in the way you respond to these events. The key is persistence, practice, and reasonable expectations for success."

In his many publications, Albert Ellis lists more forms of irrational thinking, along with strategies for correcting such beliefs. Once again, it is not necessary to completely assess all your clients for their thinking patterns; indeed, to attempt to do so might be considered an irrational expectation in itself! Simply alerting your clients to the existence of such forms of thinking, or referring them to some of the excellent literature, may be enough to insure that inappropriate attitudes and cognitive distortions do not interfere with the learning and practice of effective stress management skills.

CHAPTER 18

PROGRAM PLANNING

A properly-organized program that is based on progression, the goals of the course and the background of the group, and is adapted to the time available enhances the success of a stress management course. This chapter focuses on program planning considerations which promote smoothness and continuity. This chapter also includes a sample program outline.

PROGRAM PLANNING TIPS

We have used these general concepts with great success in many of our stress management programs. Obviously the time schedule, the facilitator's background, the clientele, and the course objectives will alter the validity of some our comments and suggestions. As you read through these suggestions, think about how they may apply and how you can alter them to fit your individual setting.

BEGIN EACH COURSE WITH THE INFORMATION, HANDOUTS AND/OR FORMS THAT SHOULD BE COMPLETED PRIOR TO THE BEGINNING OF A STRESS MANAGEMENT PROGRAM

Obtaining essential information as well as distributing handouts and filling out forms should be done early in a class to prevent the disruption of continuity. As a facilitator you should consider the following:

Take class roll

Information about the facility

location of smoking areas

location of vending machines
location of toilets
Time schedule
starting time
ending time
when to expect breaks
Assignments (if appropriate)
Overview of the course and the course
objectives
Complete necessary paperwork
registration forms
liability release forms, if necessary
pre-testing, if necessary
participant data sheets
(see Chapter 19 for information
about participant data sheets)
other forms, comments, and announcements
as needed

INCLUDE A BOUNDARY-BREAKING ACTIVITY

It is much easier for individuals to relax when they know the people around them. We've compared classes that use boundary-breaking activities and those that do not and have found that the attitude of the class is much more relaxed when we have taken the time to establish class unity.

Boundary-breaking activities are designed to accomplish several goals important to a successful stress management class.

These goals are:

1.   Boundary-breaking should be completed by the end of the first class meeting or by the time of the first break in a long class session.

2.   Class members should know each others' names at the completion of boundary-breaking activities.

A.   In classes under 30 people, each individual should know the first name of 90 to 100% of the class members.

B.   In classes over 30, each individual should know the names of and have conversed with 2 to 4 other members.

3.   The facilitator should know the first name of all group members in a class under 30.

4.   There should be no need for name tags after the boundary-breaking activities. Remember that name tags remove the personal touch and, therefore, interfere with the group cohesiveness you are trying to establish.

A variety of activities can be used to remove the barriers and allow clients to get to know each other in a non-threatening manner. The selection of activities should be based on the goals for the group as well as the time available.

The following boundary-breaking activities can be used independently or in combination:

Self-Introductions

Each person tells a little about himself or herself.

Partner Introductions

Clients pair up and spend three to ten minutes getting to know each other. (They should select someone they have not met before.) Following that conversation they form dyads. Then each person introduces his/her partner to the two people they have joined. Upon completion of this conversation, the group reconvenes and each client introduces his/her partner to the entire group.

•••••••• INSTRUCTIONAL POINTERS ••••••••

1. *Always form dyads after the original pairing. This serves a dual purpose:*

    A. *Clients get to know two other individuals in addition to their partner;*
    B. *They can practice the introduction in a less-threatening small group setting and the practice instills confidence for the large group introductions to follow.*

2. *To ensure successful partner introductions, suggest some leading questions that allow the individuals to talk about more than just the weather. Some sample questions are listed in Table 18-1.*

3. *Have clients select partners that they have not met prior to the class. This encourages them to meet someone new which is the purpose of the exercise.*

4. *Let the clients know it's O.K. to make a mistake.*

5. *Establish a maximum time limit, say thirty seconds to one minute depending on class size and time available, for the class introductions. This will remove some of the stress and apprehension that some clients have about speaking in a group (see point 6).*

6. *Begin the introductions by introducing yourself (or if team teaching, by introducing each other). By doing this you set the pace and establish the time frame.*

Circle Name Game

This is an ideal activity for classes of up to twenty-five or thirty individuals. The goal of the Circle Name Game is to get all participants to know the first name of all the others within an eight to ten minute time period.

1.   Arrange the class in a circle.

2.   Person #1 introduces him/herself (first name only). Person #2 introduces #1 and him/herself. Person #3 introduces #1, #2, and him/herself. Continue around the circle until each person has introduced him/herself, always starting with #1.

Figure 18 - 1

**The Circle Name Game
(under 25 people)**

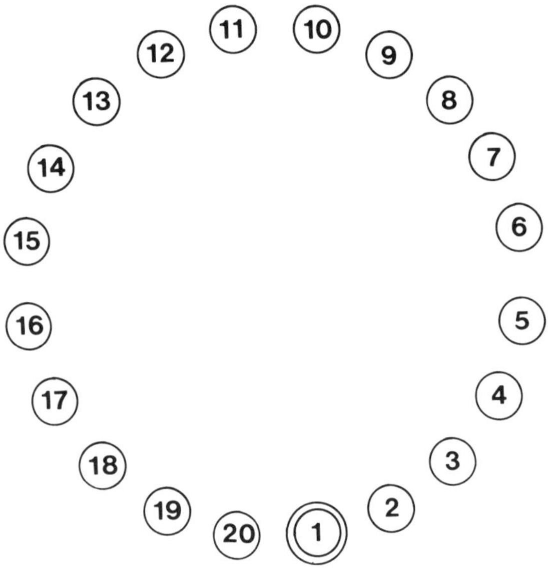

••••••••• INSTRUCTIONAL POINTERS ••••••••

1. *Emphasize that each person always starts with #1. This allows for maximum repetition, a major principle of learning.*

2. *No writing allowed. Tell participants to look at each person and to put names and faces together. This isn't possible if they are writing down the order of people.*

3. *As a facilitator, place yourself in the most strategic position in the circle. If someone appears stressed, or if it appears that they may have trouble with names, you can remove some of the tension by having them sit immediately to your left. You then begin the activity and they will follow. Keep in mind that person #20 must remember all the names of participants 1 through 19.*

4. *Have the clients go slowly so each person can make the name/face connection. As a facilitator you may have to step in occasionally to remind clients to slow down.*

5. *In a large group of twenty-five to forty, go halfway around the circle to the right, then begin again at that number (#15 in the example). This speeds up the process by cutting down on the amount of repetitions of the early names; and the activity is easier to do.*

Number 1 starts the activity and #15 finishes the first half of the activity (#1 - #15). Number 16 then begins the game over and continues to #30 who says the names of participants 16 through 30.

Figure 18 - 2

The Circle Name Game
(over 25 people)

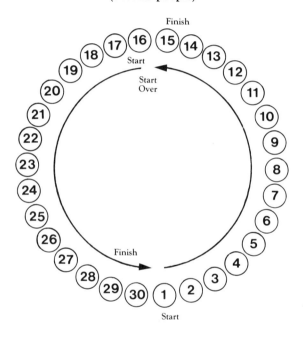

We have found that in a class of twenty to twenty-five people, with thirty-five to forty minutes allowed for boundary breaking (keep in mind that this is a 16-32 hour class), we can do the following and meet all of the goals we've established:

1. Partner introductions (with warm up sheet, three to five minutes).

Table 18 - 1
Partner Introduction Exercise
Getting To Know You

1. My name is _____

2. I am from _____

3. My occupation/title is _____

4. The most rewarding part of my job is _____

    _____

5. I control my stress by _____

6. I become irritated when _____

    _____

7. I am happiest when_____

    _____

8. When I relax I like to _____

9. When I am feeling anxious in a new situation, I _____

    _____

10. Right now I am feeling _____

2. Dyad introduction (five to six minutes). Each person has approximately one and one-half minutes to introduce his/her partner to the other two.

3. Partner introduction to entire group (ten to fifteen minutes).

4. Circle name game (ten to twelve minutes).

As a facilitator, you get to know all of the names and a little about each person's background. Group members get to know one person quite well, two more pretty well, and the first name of each person in the group. At break time, most people search out someone for further conversation, and the relaxed, friendly tone is established for the class.

THE FIRST CLASS PERIOD SHOULD ALWAYS CONTAIN AT LEAST ONE RELAXATION TECHNIQUE THAT IS DONE WELL

People sign up for a relaxation class or come to a counseling session expecting to learn how to relax. If the first class covers introductory materials, registration, forms, and theory without any relaxation techniques, people may not think the class is practical and may not return for another session. Therefore, a relaxation technique should be introduced during the first class period.

FOR BEST RESULTS ARRANGE ALL THE RELAXATION TECHNIQUES IN SEQUENTIAL ORDER (Order of Progression)

The relaxation phase of the course must be taught in sequence. Lay the foundation with basic techniques and build upon this foundation. Move to more difficult techniques only after the clients have mastered the basics.

IF A COURSE INCLUDES TOUCHING OR MASSAGE, SOME FORM OF TOUCHING SHOULD BE INCORPORATED EARLY IN THE COURSE

Many people have a difficult time touching others or being touched by others, especially if they are not well acquainted with the people involved. In this situation, any form of touching or massage may cause tension in the clients. To prevent this from occurring, incorporate some type of non-threatening touching to alleviate the sensations. You can then progress by desensitizing the clients slowly. (See Partner Sensory Awareness Technique in Chapter 7.)

•••••••••INSTRUCTIONAL POINTER•••••••••

The partner sensory awareness exercise is an excellent technique to introduce touching. It is a good technique to teach sensory awareness skills and, as a spin-off effect, it introduces touching to break down barriers that could cause difficulties later on in the course.

BEGINNING TECHNIQUES SHOULD BE KEPT SHORT. GRADUALLY INCREASE THE TIME OF THE RELAXATION TECHNIQUES AS THE CLASS PROGRESSES

People usually have the most difficulty performing a relaxation skill when they are first introduced to the technique. Many difficulties can be avoided if the time for the first practice session of a technique is kept to a minimum. Use the first time through a technique as a chance to clarify and to learn the new technique.

The second and third times through a technique should be longer than the first time. Each successive time the skill is performed, the time in the state of total relaxation (at the end of the technique) can be lengthened. The benefits to this are: first, when a new technique is introduced and tried, some people will not be quite sure how to do it. If the technique is done for five to seven minutes, it will be a waste of time for those unsure of how to do it. Secondly, many people are not familiar with the feelings involved in deep relaxation. Some of the sensations will be uncomfortable for unsuspecting clients, and they can become concerned when these feelings surface. It is better to guide them to light levels of relaxation during skills done early in a class and allow them to slowly progress to deeper and deeper levels. Thus, they get used to the sensations slowly.

• • • • • • • • • INSTRUCTIONAL POINTER • • • • • • • • •

We suggest doing each technique several times. For example, after you introduce a technique, lead the clients into a relaxed state for two to three minutes. (You may want to shorten a longer technique the first time through.) Give them very little time at the end of the exercise for deepening the relaxation. Have the clients come out of the technique and process or discuss it. (See the next paragraph.) Answer any questions the clients have and, if necessary, reintroduce the skill. Then repeat the technique and allow more time to deepen relaxation at the end. Process the technique a second time and repeat again if necessary.

PROCESS EACH RELAXATION SKILL DONE IN CLASS

One of the best learning methods employed in a relaxation class is the discussion that takes place after each technique. Each period of relaxation should be processed. Discussion items during this period should range from problems or difficulties encountered, sensations and feelings they are having, concerns they have and, in general, anything and everything the clients want to discuss related to the technique or the course.

A tremendous amount of learning takes place during the

processing of a technique. Some clients share sensations they've felt and how they've responded. Then you can encourage others to search for these feelings as you repeat the skill. Many people are reassured when they learn that others have a concern or a feeling similiar to theirs. If there is a difficulty or concern, a facilitator can clarify what is happening and accentuate the positive. Many questions about relaxation that could never be built into a course outline will come up in the discussions. This also helps give the clients a feeling of control over the direction of the course.

• • • • • • • • • INSTRUCTIONAL POINTERS • • • • • • • •

1.	*Process each skill. Ask the clients what they felt, what was new or different, comfortable or uncomfortable, what worked, what didn't, what problems they had, etc. After processing, repeat the skill, if necessary, and process it again. Always process each and every relaxation skill.*

2.	*Questions that come up in the discussions will vary considerably and may lead to coverage of diverse topics such as hypnosis, imagery, sleep, etc. Yet we've found that some questions appear during most classes. In Chapter 5 we've listed the most commonly asked questions and possible responses or answers.*

ARRANGE THE SCHEDULE OF ACTIVITIES SO THAT RELAXATION PRACTICE ALTERNATES WITH BREAKS, FILMS, LECTURES, SMALL GROUP ACTIVITIES OR EXERCISE

Too much relaxation can be stressful. It can also inhibit client satisfaction with the class. This is especially true if the clients are not used to sitting quietly and relaxing. We have found that a maximum of ten to fifteen minutes of actual relaxation should be allotted at any one time. After processing, engage the class in some other activity and return to relaxation later. (See the sample program outline at the end of this chapter for ideas on how to vary relaxation practice with other components.)

IF POSSIBLE, INCORPORATE SOME TYPE OF PHYSICAL ACTIVITY INTO A CLASS THAT MEETS FOR MORE THAN ONE HOUR.

Exercise is an important component of a stress management program. That may seem paradoxical because exercise is a stressor. However, after exercise the body rebounds to a relaxed state. Therefore you should emphasize, whether through information or physical activity, the importance of exercise in any stress management program.

It is equally important for an individual to move about and increase body awareness during a relaxation class. If a person relaxes too much during any one period of time, body awareness diminishes and it becomes more difficult for the client to sense and feel the sensations associated with relaxation. Finally, pent-up emotions and built up energy need to be decreased or clients begin fidgeting and become restless.

•••••••••INSTRUCTIONAL POINTERS••••••••

1. *During breaks, encourage or require clients to take a walk or to engage in some type of exercise.*

2. *During class, have clients stand and stretch to dissipate some of their built-up energy.*

ONCE RELAXATION HAS BEEN INTRODUCED, BEGIN AND END EACH CLASS WITH A REVIEW AND A RELAXATION TECHNIQUE

There are several reasons for beginning and ending each class session with a review and a relaxation technique. The review is important to refresh what has been covered in the previous sessions and to outline what will be introduced during the upcoming class. At the end of the class, review what has been learned during that class period. In other words, let the clients know what they've already learned, what they are about to learn, and, at the end of the class, review with them what they have just learned. As simple as it seems, this repetition reinforces the key points you want the clients to learn.

The relaxation techniques incorporated at the beginning and end of each class are also important to the goals of the class. Relaxation techniques incorporated at these times:

1. help reduce or remove anxiety of the clients at the start of each class;

2. help slow down the clients early in the class thus setting the tone for the class;

3. allow clients to leave feeling relaxed; and

4. ensure that the clients are relaxing at least twice during that day.

• • • • • • • • • INSTRUCTIONAL POINTER • • • • • • • • •

Be sure to emphasize to clients how to reinvigorate themselves at the end of a class. This is especially important for clients who may be driving since, if they do not reinvigorate themselves, deep relaxation may leave them a bit groggy for ten to fifteen minutes.

PLAN AN ACTIVITY OTHER THAN RELAXATION IMME-DIATELY FOLLOWING LUNCH BREAKS

Relaxation techniques can redirect the blood flow in the body away from the internal organs to the extremities. If done immediately after eating this could slow down the digestion process. Therefore, it is recommended that you refrain from relaxation for at least one hour if possible. This suggestion is not carved in granite but is a good general policy to adhere to and, with advance planning, can be incorporated quite easily into your schedule. (See page 37 for more information on this topic.)

•••••••• INSTRUCTIONAL POINTER ••••••••

Encourage participants to eat a light meal prior to or during a stress management class, especially when total body relaxation techniques are going to be introduced.

THE GOAL OF THE COURSE, THE CLASS MAKE-UP AND THE TIME FRAME DETERMINE WHAT CAN BE OR SHOULD BE INCLUDED IN A CLASS

As a facilitator, plan for the most appropriate components for the group as a whole. We believe that all clients should recognize the importance of a holistic approach to stress management. Relaxation by itself is not a cure-all. In fact, for many clients it may be used as a bandaid to cover up or mask a greater problem. Present a well-organized program that includes components that address the source of stress and the most desirable intervention strategies to effectively deal with stress.

Components that can be used include, but are not limited to, the following:

Sensory awareness
Breathing techniques
Supporting environment exercises
Imagination skills

Practical relaxation skills
Communication skills
  (including assertiveness)
Time management
  (including goal setting and
  establishing priorities)
Exercise
Cognitive restructuring of thoughts
Development of support persons
Self acceptance
Humor
Leisure, hobbies and other diversions

INTRODUCE A VARIETY OF TECHNIQUES USING BOTH PATHWAYS TO RELAXATION

Always remember that each person is unique and may learn differently than others in the class. What works for one person may not work for another. Since there are two categories of relaxation techniques, be sure to include exercises from each group. That is, introduce a variety of relaxation techniques so that each person can benefit by finding skills that work best for him or her (See Chapter 10 for more information on the two pathways to relaxation.)

OVERPLAN - AND ADAPT TO THE GROUP

When first beginning to teach relaxation classes, be prepared to present plenty of material to the group but let the class establish the pace. You don't have to cover everything you've planned for the class but it is nice to have enough material if needed. You will find that the clients may use more time than you've scheduled for discussions and questions.

• • • • • • • • • INSTRUCTIONAL POINTERS • • • • • • • •

1. You, as the facilitator, should adapt to the class - never have the class adapt to you and your pace.

2. NEVER RUSH! Rushing is contrary to what you are trying to do in a relaxation class. Take your time and cover the information thoroughly.

KEEP IT SIMPLE AND REPEAT, REPEAT, REPEAT!

Repetition is a major principle of learning. Repeat information as often as needed. It is better to cover less information and repeat it until the clients understand it and know how to perform those techniques well rather than to introduce many additional techniques which they never learn to perform properly.

BE CAREFUL WITH THE IMAGINATION TECHNIQUES IN A CLASS

Do not introduce imagination techniques too early in a class. In addition, be sure to introduce them well so as to prevent problems. If a problem is going to occur with clients in a relaxation class, it usually occurs during imagination exercises. Therefore, it is important to take extra caution in selecting techniques as well as to properly prepare the clients for the imagination techniques. Before introducing any imagination techniques make sure you are qualified to do so.(See Chapter 11 on visualization.)

• • • • • • • • • INSTRUCTIONAL POINTER • • • • • • • • •

The larger the class and the less you know about the individuals in a class, the greater the caution you should exercise with imagination techniques.

SAMPLE PROGRAM OUTLINE

This sample outline illustrates how the principles covered in this chapter can be worked into a stress management program. The outline is an example of a two day, sixteen hour workshop, but the principles can be worked into any time frame. The outline is presented here strictly as an example, not as a recommendation.

The outline need not be followed exactly as illustrated. The facilitator should adapt it to the group according to the client's ability to grasp the information presented.

SAMPLE PROGRAM OUTLINE - STRESS MANAGEMENT WORKSHOP

DAY ONE

COURSE INTRODUCTION
Instructor introduction
Class roll
Introduction to the facility
Course overview
Participant data sheet
Assignments, grading

COMPONENTS OF A RELAXATION PROGRAM (The Holistic Approach to Relaxation)

BOUNDARY-BREAKING ACTIVITY
Partner introduction game
Circle name game

DINNER BREAK (Eat a light meal and get some exercise)

INTRODUCTION TO STRESS
What is stress
Benefits of relaxation

POINTS TO KEEP IN MIND AND BASIC RELAXATION
POSITIONS

SENSORY AWARENESS EXERCISES

Individual sensory awareness
Partner sensory awareness

SUPPORTING ENVIRONMENT EXERCISE

BREAK

INTRODUCTION TO THE BREATHING RHYTHM

The exhalation exercise
The exhalation exercise (tape)

REVIEW

DAY TWO

QUESTION/ANSWER PERIOD

REVIEW PREVIOUS EXERCISES

INTRODUCTION TO THE IMAGINATION

Chevreul's pendulum
Relaxed scenes technique
Waves and tides technique
Long breath exercise

BREAK

TIME MANAGEMENT INTRODUCTION: FILM *(The Time
Of Your Life)*

Time management discussion
Goals, prioritizing list

RELAXATION RESPONSE TECHNIQUE

THE SENSORY AWARENESS TECHNIQUE

LUNCH BREAK

THE COMMUNICATION CYCLE
Communication breakdowns and stress
Communication exercise

IMAGINATION
Long breath technique
The box technique
The hanger technique

TIME MANAGEMENT: FILM *(The Perfectly Normal Day)*
Film processing
Filing systems/organization

HEAVINESS EXERCISE—STANDARD AUTOGENIC TRAINING

INSTANT RELAXATION TECHNIQUES

REVIEW/QUESTIONS AND ANSWERS/SUMMARY

RELAXATION—CLIENTS CHOOSE TECHNIQUE AND DO IT ON THEIR OWN

CHAPTER 19

PARTICIPANT DATA INFORMATION

Clients come for stress management training from a variety of backgrounds. Facilitators of stress management classes should keep in mind that each client brings with him or her a variety of past experiences, medical conditions, and expectations for the class. One way to learn about these crucial bits of information is to have clients complete a participant data sheet prior to the beginning of stress management training. Information from such a sheet can reduce the amount of unexpected surprises for the facilitator and even help prepare the facilitator for potential emergencies. For example, knowing beforehand that one of the clients is an epileptic allows the facilitator to prepare for emergency conditions (i.e., a seizure) and to control classroom conditions better.

Participant data sheets are as individualized as the facilitator who is leading a stress management class or working with a client. There is no one form that covers all the necessary background information. If the facilitator is functioning within a medical service system, such as a hospital or neighborhood health clinic, the medical system may already require that specific information be collected before the client can receive care. In this situation the facilitator may need only a brief form to address information specific to the facilitator's needs. If the facilitator is leading stress management classes at a site where little information is collected prior to the class (e.g., educational settings at a school, YMCA, or nursing home), more extensive information will need to be collected.

The participant data form should collect only that information which the facilitator plans to use and which has not already been collected elsewhere. A brief, specific form speeds the work of the facilitator and does not use excessive time at the beginning of the stress management training program.

PARTICIPANT IDENTIFICATION INFORMATION

Information in this category aids the facilitator in identifying the client. Data such as name, sex, business and home address, business and home telephone number, occupation, social security number, date of birth, hospital records number, and Medicare/Medicaid identification number all fall into this category. Such information should provide the facilitator with a quick and easy method to retrieve basic information about the stress management client and allow cross-checking of information with other sources.

STRESS SYMPTOMOLOGY

Clients often come to stress management classes or to a stress management facilitator because certain symptoms of their stress have become too obvious to ignore. They may be regular headaches linked to stressful job-related events or excessive muscle tension and pain in the shoulders and neck. Although all of these symptoms should first be examined by a health care provider to rule out physiological causes unrelated to stress, the client's self-reported information about stress symptoms can be very enlightening. The facilitator can use this important information to point to the client's body systems which tend to manifest the stress reactions the most. Certain clients may respond to tensions by tightening neck and shoulder muscles while other clients may get extremely cold hands. Other clients may have a racing heartbeat or digestive upset. The facilitator can cue clients to their reactive body systems during stress management training to help them discover the effectiveness of such training.

Data can be collected for this category via a symptom checklist, multiple choice questions, or with simple open-ended questions.

The authors prefer a symptom checklist with a few open-ended questions to ensure completeness and brevity.

MEDICAL INFORMATION

Every client comes to stress management training with a medical background that could be critical to know. Medical problems do not simply disappear during stress management training. The more informed the faciliator is about the specific medical conditions of the clients, the better prepared he or she is for potential emergencies. Clients with heart or blood vessel diseases, epilepsy, psychiatric problems, diabetes, or asthma may have an acute episode of their medical condition in the middle of stress management training. The well-prepared facilitator knows who these people are and what care they should receive.

To ensure that appropriate care is possible for acute emergencies, all clients should report the following information on the participant data sheet: (1) whether they have any medical or psychological condition which could become acute or create an emergency situation, (2) whether they are presently receiving medical or psychological help, and for what condition, (3) the names and addresses of the professionals from which they are receiving care, (4) the names of any over-the-counter and prescribed drugs they are currently taking, and the medical condition for which they are taking them, and (5) the name and address of their physician or health clinic.

Another reason for collecting background medical information from clients is to be cognizant of potential interaction between stress management training and client medical conditions. There are many examples of this effect. The physiological condition of low blood pressure can be exacerbated through stress management training to the point where the client feels dizzy and weak. This is especially true if the client is sitting upright while attempting to relax. A client with low blood sugar levels may also experience distressing symptoms during relaxation as the relaxed body becomes more efficient in sugar metabolism. A client with a psychological problem may actually use muscle tension as an armoring technique to deal with his or her condition. Removing this defensive mechanism through muscle relaxation may allow the psychological problems to resurface and manifest themselves acutely in the training session. Individuals with chronic pain from lower back pain, arthritis, or severe headaches may find that the reduced stimuli training environment for stress management allows them to focus more strongly on the pain sensations. All of these examples point to the important fact that stress management facilitators need to understand how stress management training may interact with the medical and psychological conditions of clients.

A problem/symptoms checklist, as shown in Figure 19-1, can provide a brief method for collecting background medical data and stress symptomology. It can alert the facilitator to areas of clients' medical background that need further exploration. The For Interviewer Use box in the upper right allows for a quick and condensed picture of the client when meeting with the client in future sessions. The CV symbol and space allows a brief note regarding cardiovascular diseases. The CN symbol and space allows a brief note about nervous system symptomology (e.g., cold hands, racing heart) or if the client is prone to convulsions. The HYPO symbol and space allows comment for conditions of low blood pressure or low blood sugar levels (and if the patient is diabetic), while the HYPR symbol and space allows a note if the subject is hypertensive. The MED symbol provides a brief space for noting whether the client is taking medications that might interact with the physiological alterations due to relaxation. The Greek symbol, psi, can be circled if the client has had, or is having, psychological or psychiatric problems.

Again, the medical information is meant to prepare the stress management facilitator for medical emergencies or acute medical episodes which may or may not occur. The facilitator who is

Figure 19 - 1

CONFIDENTIAL CONFIDENTIAL CONFIDENTIAL

Brief Medical Background Survey

(For Interviewer Use)
CV: ________ HYPO: ______/______: HYPR
CN: ________ MED: Ψ

Name:

Date:

Directions: Please indicate if you have experienced any of the following symptoms or problems in the past or present. If you respond *yes* to any problem or symptom, please give a brief explanation of your present or past condition.

Yes, presently	**Yes, in the past**	**No**	**Problem/Symptom**	**Brief Explanation**
			Heart or blood vessel diseases	
			Tension, migraine or cluster headaches	
			High or low blood pressure	
			Diabetes/blood sugar disorders	
			Asthma/lung diseases	
			Stomach/digestive system diseases	
			Thyroid or other gland diseases	
			Cancer/benign tumors	
			Arthritis/bone or joint disorders	
			Epilepsy/dizziness or fainting spells	
			Numbness or tingling in extremities	
			Skin rashes or disorders	
			Allergies to medications or substances	
			Insomnia/sleep difficulties	
			Inability to concentrate	
			Psychological/psychiatric problems	
			Depression	
			Pain (shooting, dull, nagging)	
			Chronically tired/exhausted	
			Other (not mentioned above)	

continued

A.   Are you presently receiving any professional help for medical or psychological problems? ☐Yes   ☐ No
      If Yes, Name of Professional:
      Form of Practice:
      City, State of Practice:

B.   Are you currently taking any prescribed or over-the-counter medications?
      ☐ Yes   ☐ No
      If Yes, Name of Medication(s):
      Condition Medication is for:

C.   Name of Family Physician:
      City, State of Practice:

D.   Any further conditions you would like us to know about?

unaware that a client is prone to fainting spells may not be much consolation to that client if he injures himself during a fainting spell.

PARTICIPANT EXPECTATIONS AND INDIVIDUAL INTERESTS

Collecting client expectations of and interests in stress management before the training begins is good educational practice. With a few initial questions, the facilitator can learn how to individualize training so that the content becomes relevant to the needs, situations, and background of the client. In a group setting, knowing the specific expectations and interests of the group of clients will help the facilitator determine how much time to spend in specific areas of content and technique and what additional sidetracks could enhance the enjoyment of the group experience. Collecting pertinent information about clients' background experiences in stress management training, exposure to stressors, and self-perceived abilities to handle those stressors can help the facilitator gauge how advanced the training should be. The following sample questions provide basic information in this category:

What are three specific expectations or areas of interest you have about this stress management training program?

How do you currently handle your stressors? How successful are you?

Have you received prior training in stress management? If yes, what?

Please complete this statement. By the end of this stress management training program, I want to . . .

A FINAL NOTE

Since anonymity cannot be assured with a participant data form, confidentiality of information becomes a vital issue. The information should be collected, stored, and disposed of in ways that ensure confidentiality. The data should be shared only with personnel involved in the stress management skills training of the client.

CHAPTER 20

PROPER USE OF
AUDIOVISUAL EQUIPMENT

Even though facilitators may have the knowledge and the background to conduct excellent classes, the classes may fall short of client expectations because the material is not professionally or properly presented. Research indicates that the proper use of audiovisual support can greatly increase the professionalism, the impact of the material, and the understanding and retention of the participants.[1] This chapter discusses why the presentation is important and how to use selected audiovisual materials.

WHY COMMUNICATION FAILS

Communication is a complicated process. Effective communication means turning a thought or feeling into a message, and transmitting that message to another person so that the person interprets the message as intended. The message is transmitted to the receiver by word symbols, body postures and gestures, and voice fluctuations, tones and pitch. The message then travels visually or through sound waves.[2]

Too often, we place too much emphasis on only one means of communication...*words*. We rely on words when we tell people something and provide them with written materials. As indicated in Chapter 2, words account for only about 7% of a transmitted message. Overreliance on words leads to verbalism and forgetting because words which are filled with meaning for one person may be devoid of meaning for another. A person must carry meaning to a word before he or she can carry meaning from that word.[3]

Unless the meaning of words is absolutely clear to us, we need help beyond words to acquire long-term knowledge. If words are not enough for effective communication, we must find techniques which emphasize the meaning. The proper use of good visual support is helpful. Not only does the visual support help clarify what's important but, when used properly, they also can be effective in clarifying information to large groups of people.

ADVANCE PREPARATION

Regardless of the type of visual aids to be used to clarify or to make a point, certain requirements should be met prior to the class.

ELECTRICAL OUTLETS

Check for the location and type of electrical outlets in the room.

• • • • • • • • • INSTRUCTIONAL POINTER • • • • • • • • •

Be sure that the outlets are 3 prong or be sure to bring a 3 prong to 2 prong adapter. Most audiovisual equipment requires a 3 prong outlet.

ROOM ARRANGEMENT AND ADVANCE SET-UP

Set up proper seating arrangement. Be sure that the room can accommodate visual support and other props if they are to be used.

When planning seating, do so to encourage discussion and be sure everyone has a clear view of the leader.

Determine appropriate placement of the projector in the room as well as placement of the screen to ensure that everyone can see the screen as well as the facilitator. (See page 247 for more information.)

Learn where and how lights are controlled in the room.

Have handout materials ready and appropriately placed in the room.

Arrange audiovisual materials in proper sequence and in proper position within the room.

Rehearse.[4]

• • • • • • • • • INSTRUCTIONAL POINTER • • • • • • • • •

Rehearse the transition between lecture and the use of visual support as well as the actual use of these materials.

MEDIA SUPPORT CHECKLIST

Figure 20-1, The Audiovisual Checklist, may be helpful to you when planning and preparing for a presentation. Obviously, the list must be adapted to fit your needs. However, when making a presentation (especially when unfamiliar with the room) we have found that it always pays to be overprepared for possile problems when using audiovisual equipment. We encourage you to copy it and adapt it for your use.

OVERHEAD PROJECTORS

One of the most useful of audiovisual supports is the overhead projector. Research done at the University of Pennsylvania found that presenters who used the overhead projector and transparencies were "perceived as significantly better prepared, more professional, more persuasive, more highly credible and more interesting" than presenters that did not use the overhead.

The study also found that, when using the overhead projector to clarify information and to make points, group decisions were reached faster and meetings were shorter. In addition, it was found that the time spent in lengthy monologues was reduced and that verbal exchanges were increased - a process that communications experts regard as an important characteristic of effective communications.[5] With these results, it is easy to see why overhead projectors are a commonly used audiovisual aid.

Figure 20 - 1

Audiovisual Checklist

Equipment

✔ if needed	✔ when packed	
☐	☐*	Screen
☐	☐*	Slide Projector
☐	☐	extra bulb for slide projector
☐	☐	remote extension for slide projector
☐	☐*	Overhead Projector
☐	☐	extra bulb for overhead projector
☐	☐	marking pencils (grease or felt) for transparencies
☐	☐	blank transparencies
☐	☐*	16 mm Projector
☐	☐	extra bulb for 16 mm projector
☐	☐	take up reel (check for proper size)
☐	☐	Electrical outlet adapters (3 prong to 2 prong) 2 minimum
☐	☐	Extension Cords (check for proper size *and* length) 2 minimum

Materials

Slide Trays (name of tray / topic needed)

☐ _____

☐ _____

☐ _____

Films (title of films)

☐ _____

☐ _____

☐ _____

Overhead Transparencies (name/title of transparencies needed)

☐ _____

☐ _____

☐ _____

☐ _____

☐ _____

*Check working order before packing.

ADVANTAGES OF THE OVERHEAD PROJECTOR

There are many advantages to using the overhead projector. The list below includes some of the main advantages.

It complements the facilitator's efforts whereas most other projection techniques tend to replace the instructor.

It can be used in a fully-illuminated room so there is no need to darken the room.

The image is large and bright so that attention is attracted and held to the screen.

The facilitator faces the audience at all times. This makes it easier to control the volume of the voice, maintain eye contact, obtain continuous non-verbal feedback, and make on-the-spot adjustments in the presentation if necessary.

The facilitator has complete control of the material at all times.

It's easy to adjust the size of the screen images so that everyone can see them.

The facilitator can write on, point to, underline, etc., to emphasize or clarify or simply to hold the client's attention.

The projector is easy to operate and relatively inexpensive.

The facilitator can provide duplicates of the transparencies in handout form (clients can follow along, take notes on the handouts, etc.).

The image is projected high enough so the facilitator and the projector do not block the view.

Transparencies can be prepared ahead and they can be quickly removed once their purpose is over.

Transparencies can save presentation time. They eliminate repetitive chalkboard work.

Transparencies can be mounted on 10-inch by 12-inch (outside dimension) frames which fit standard filing drawers.

TEACHING TIPS FOR USING THE OVERHEAD PROJECTOR

When using the overhead projector, *do not* read from the screen. Read the material from the transparency itself. This allows the facilitator to face the audience at all times which is a major advantage over using a chalkboard.

Consider using a pointer to direct the clients' attention to material on the transparency. *Never point to the screen*, only point to the transperancy.

• • • • • • • • INSTRUCTIONAL POINTERS • • • • • • • • •

1. *Place the pointer directly on the transparency so that movements of the pointer (hand) will not be exaggerated.*

2. *Add detail to a transparency with a felt or a wax-based pen.*

3. *You can cover the transparency with a clear plastic sheet to write on so that the original is not marred.*

4. *Use paper or cardboard to cover all or part of a transparency. This way you can progressively disclose information. You can build up to the key points without overwhelming the audience with a completely full screen from the start.*

5. *Thin white paper can be used to cover a transparency in order to prevent the image from going to the screen but still permit you to see the image so that you will know what's coming next.*

6. Whenever possible, mount your transparencies on the 10-inch by 12-inch mounting frames. As mentioned previously, this is a standard size that fits into standard filing drawers. In addition, the mounting frame protects the transparencies and makes them easier to read on the screen. The mounting frame concentrates the light by cutting down on extraneous light; this focuses the clients' attention to the material on the screen.

7. Place your notes, cues, title, etc. on the mounting border. No one but you will be able to see them.[6]

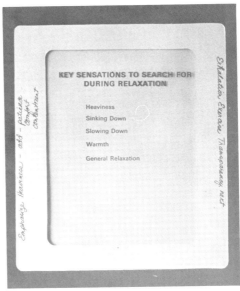

8. Use the on/off technique to direct attention either to information on the screen or to you. This is an important point and should be kept constantly in mind. A transparency that's projected on the screen when it is not needed competes for the client's attention while the facilitator attempts to teach.

PROJECTOR PLACEMENT

Set up the projector and screen in the most strategic position in the room. While most people set up the screen and overhead projector in the middle of the front of the room, this placement obscures the vision of the majority of people in the room. Proper placement allows clear vision for the majority of clients. Figure 20-2 shows five excellent ways to position the screen and the projector in a room to allow for maximum viewing.

Figure 20 - 2

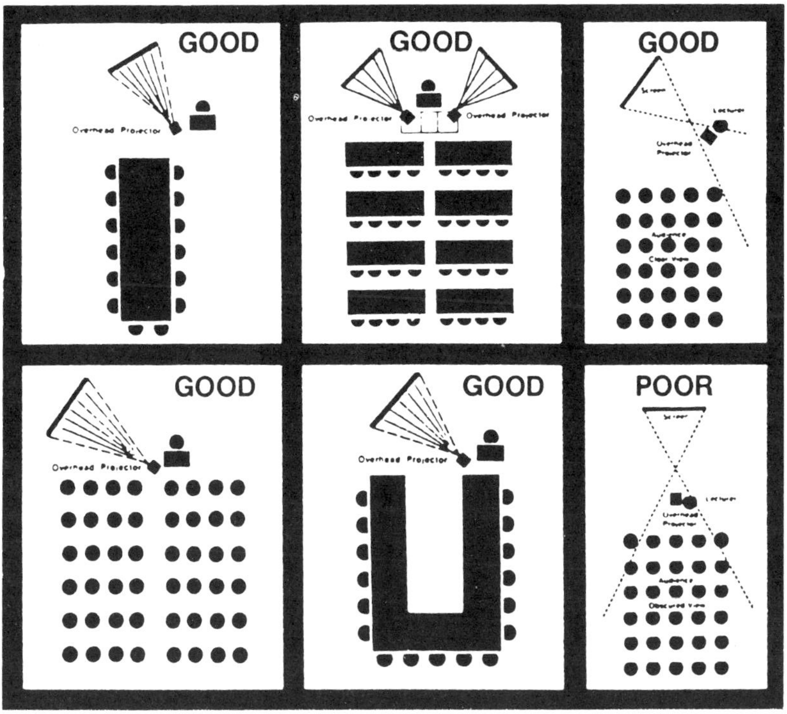

Used with the permission of the 3M Corporation.[7]

BASIC TIPS FOR MAKING TRANSPARENCIES

Use simple, not complex, letters when making transparencies.

Generally avoid type styles with serifs.

Titles should be short and typed in capital letters.

Proper spacing between letters and words is important for ease of reading.

Each transparency should illustrate only one point.

Avoid cramming too much text onto a transparency. Too much information and detail will confuse the clients and detract from the presentation.

When possible, use illustrations instead of text and develop your talk around the illustrations.

When making transparencies follow these rules to allow for maximum viewing with minimum effort:

A maximum of 9 lines per transparency

A maximum of 6 or 7 words per line

A minimum of 24 point type for the title

A minimum of 14 point type for the information on a page.

A maximum of 1/8 inch thickness for solid black lines.[8,9]

SLIDE PROJECTORS, 16MM FILMS AND CHALKBOARDS

THE USE OF SLIDES

The slide projector is another useful way to present visual aids. There are advantages and disadvantages in using a slide projector and slides.

Advantages of Using Slides

Slides can be prepared professionally and in advance.

Photographs are clearly projected from slides.

Slides can be programmed easily. The facilitator determines the order and the transfer of the audience's attention.

During a presentation, slides can be changed with less fuss than overhead transparencies.

As a facilitator you can develop a mini-lecture for each slide. The slides then serve as reminders that keep your presentation in order.

A presentation can be adapted easily by adding and deleting slides.

Disadvantages of Slides

The major disadvantage of using slides is that they require advance preparation. The layout, set-up, graphics work and photo/development may take one to three weeks to produce the finished slides.

•••••••••• INSTRUCTIONAL POINTERS ••••••••

1.   *When using slides, it is a good idea to have a remote extension available to advance the slides. The average remote control cord allows you to move about six to eight feet from the projector. A twenty to fifty foot remote extension will allow you to operate the projector from the front of a room rather than the back. Remote extensions are relatively inexpensive. Most can be purchased for $15.00 to $30.00 depending on their length. If you use slides at all, the remote extension will make your presentations go much smoother.*

2.   *It is also helpful to put blank cardboard slides in appropriate places in the slide tray so you can direct attention away from the slides. This allows the clients' attention to focus from the slide image to a darkened screen (as if the projector is off) and to you, the facilitator. Thus, you can interrupt slide viewing and return to it without turning the machine off.*

3.   *Always place a blank cardboard slide at the start and the end of slides so that there are no "white outs" on the screen. This will increase the professionalism of a presentation.*

USING FILMS

The popularity of films has increased in recent years due to the large number and excellent quality available. Regardless of the topic, somewhere there is a high caliber film that could be used. As with all forms of media support equipment, there are some key points to remember when using films.

Proper Use of Films

Advance selection and preparation: For maximum potential from a film, the facilitator must do his or her part in advance selection and preparation. Keep in mind that films move rapidly and if the viewers take their eyes off the screen, even for a short period, they are likely to miss something. Listed below are some key points to remember when using films:

Proper film selection is important. *Never* develop a class around a film because the film is a good one. Determine the objectives of your class first and then select films based on your objectives.

Preview all films before showing them. The facilitator must be thoroughly acquainted with its contents if the film is going to be an effective teaching tool. As you preview it, take notes, read the film guide, develop your own questions, list key points and the like. The Film Evaluation Form (Figure 20-3) may be useful for preparing to use a film in a class.

Figure 20-3

Film Evaluation Form

Topic _____

Title _____

Grade Level _____

Color_____ B&W_____ Length (min.) _____

Copyright Date _____ Rental Cost_____

Purchasing Cost _____ Catalogue Order # _____

Catalogue Order # _____ Rental Address _____

Purchasing Address _____ _____

_____

	Low 1	2	3	4	High 5
Vocabulary	—	—	—	—	—
Up-to-Date	—	—	—	—	—
Realistic	—	—	—	—	—
Student Interest	—	—	—	—	—
Overall Rating	—	—	—	—	—

Description of Content:

Introductory Questions / Comments:

Follow-Up Activities:

Additional Comments (strengths, weaknesses, etc.):

Properly prepare the group for viewing. Discuss what is already known about the subject and explain what they (the clients) can learn from viewing the film. You may want to list key words on the board as well as a list of key questions to be answered by the film. (List them in sequential order according to their use in the film.)

Have some type of planned follow-up activities and discussion. Discuss what was examined in the film, re-emphasize the key points and/or practice the skills taught in the film if appropriate. The facilitator's film guide that accompanies many films can be useful in planning follow-up questions and activities.[10]

·········INSTRUCTIONAL POINTERS········

1.   *If during projecture the film begins jumping, the loop restoration can be done by pressing the "loop restorer" and holding it down for a few seconds before releasing it, placing the projector in reverse for a few seconds or by manually rebuilding the loop.*

2.   *Since films "move" quickly, note taking may cause the viewers to miss important material. To discourage note taking provide handouts with the outline and key points of the film so the clients can focus on the film itself when viewing it.*

USING CHALKBOARDS

Chalkboards and dry-erase boards are available in most rooms where classes are taught and are an obvious and widely used form of media support. The use of the chalkboard is pretty obvious but once again, there are some key points that can make its use more effective.

Keep writing brief and to the point.

When writing on the board, turn back to the group and ask questions to keep them alert.

To prevent writing up or down hill on the board, place several dots on the board before the class begins.

Write key points outline, etc., on the board beforehand and go to the back of the room to check it out for clarity. To be seen clearly the board must be properly lighted, the chalk color must contrast with the board, letters must be large enough and the spacing between letters and words must be adequate.

•••••••• INSTRUCTIONAL POINTER ••••••••

Before a class write relevant material on the board and cover it by taping paper over it or by pulling a screen down. Then it can be uncovered at the appropriate time during the class.

FOOTNOTES

CHAPTER 1

1. D. Bernstein & T. Borkovec (1977). *Progressive Relaxation Training: A Manual for the Helping Professions.* (Champaign: Research Press), p. 17.

CHAPTER 2

1. J. Curtis & R. Detert (1981). *How to Relax: A Holistic Approach to Stress Managment.* (Palo Alto: Mayfield), p. 178.

2. D. Bernstein & T. Borkovec (1977). *Progressive Relaxation Training: A Manual for the Helping Professions.* (Champaign: Research Press), pp. 31-32.

3. Ibid.

CHAPTER 3

1. D. Bernstein & T. Borkovec (1977). *Progressive Relaxation Training: A Manual for the Helping Professions.* (Champaign: Research Press), pp. 52-53.

CHAPTER 4

1. J. Greenberg (1983). *Comprehensive Stress Management.* (Dubuque, Iowa: William C. Brown Co. Publishers), p. 21.

2. S. Appelbaum (1981). *Stress Management for Health Care Professionals.* (Rockville, Maryland: Aspen Publication), p. 77.

3. Adapted from mimeographed handout, source unknown.

4. Adapted from mimeographed handout, source unknown.

CHAPTER 5

1. J. Curtis & R. Detert (1985). *Learn To Relax: A 14-Day Program.* (La Crosse: Coulee Press), pp. 58-61.

CHAPTER 6

1. J. Curtis & R. Detert (1985). *Learn To Relax: A 14-Day Program.* (La Crosse: Coulee Press), pp. 27-29.

2. Ibid., pp. 30-38.

CHAPTER 7

1. B. Jencks (1974). *Respiration for Relaxation, Invigoration, and Special Accomplishments.* (Salt Lake City: Private Printing), p. 10.

2. J. Curtis & R. Detert (1981). *How To Relax: A Holistic Approach to Stress Management.* (Palo Alto: Mayfield), p.72.

3. B. Jencks (1974), p. 21.

4. J. Curtis & R. Detert (1981), pp. 74-81

CHAPTER 9

1. J. Curtis & R. Detert (1981). *How To Relax: A Holistic Approach to Stress Management.* (Palo Alto: Mayfield), p. 94.

CHAPTER 10

1. C. Hampden-Turner (1981). *Maps of the Mind.* (New York: Collier.)

2. D. Girdano & G. Everly (1979). *Controlling Stress and Tension: A Holistic Approach.* (Englewood Cliffs: Prentice-Hall), p. 32.

3. J. Hoffman, et al. (1982). Reduced sympathetic nervous system responsivity associated with the relaxation response. *Science,* (215, 8 January 1982), pp. 190-192.

CHAPTER 11

1. M. Scarf (1980). Images that heal: A doubtful idea whose time has come. *Psychology Today,* 14, 32-46.

2. O. Simonton & S. Matthews-Simonton (1978). *Getting Well Again.* (New York: St. Martin's Press.)

3. O.C. Simonton & S. Matthews-Simonton (1975). Belief systems and management of the emotional aspects of malignancy. *Journal of Transpersonal Psychology,* 7 (1), 29-48.

4. K. Pelletier (1977). *Mind As Healer, Mind As Slayer.* (New York: Dell), pp. 149, 252-262.

5. G. Jampolsky (1984). *Attitudinal Healing.* Seminar conducted at the Southern Illinois University School of Medicine, Springfield, Illinois.

6. G. Jampolsky (1983). *Teach Only Love.* (New York: Bantam.)

7. B. Jencks (1977). *Your Body: Biofeedback At Its Best.* (Chicago: Nelson-Hall), pp. 25-41.

8. B. Jencks (1974). *Respiration For Relaxation, Invigoration, and Special Accomplishments.* (Salt Lake City: Private Printing.)

9. B. Jencks (1977).

10. Ibid.

11. J. Switras (1978). An alternative-form instrument to assess vividness and controllability of imagery in seven modalities. *Perceptual and Motor Skills,* 46, 379-384.

12. B. Jencks (1977), p. 30.

13. Ibid., p. 26.

14. J. Curtis & R. Detert (1981). *How To Relax: A Holistic Approach to Stress Management.* (Palo Alto: Mayfield), p. 41.

15. B. Jencks (1973). *Exercise Manual For J. H. Schultz's Standard Autogenic Training and Special Formulas.* (Salt Lake City: Private Printing), p. 22.

16. B. Jencks (1974).

17. B. Jencks (1977).

18. J. Curtis & R. Detert (1981), p. 139.

19. Ibid., p. 140.

20. Ibid., p. 145.

21. Ibid., p. 145.

22. Ibid., p. 146.

CHAPTER 12

1. D. Goleman (1977). *The Varieties of the Meditative Experience.* (New York: E.P. Dutton), p. 109.

2. K. Pelletier (1977). *Mind as Healer, Mind as Slayer.* (New York: Dell), p. 192.

3. R. Dass (1971). *Remember: Be Here Now.* (New York: Crown), p. 80.

4. R: Ornstein (1977). *The Psychology of Consciousness(2nd ed.).* (New York: Harcourt Brace Jovanovich.)

5. D. Shapiro (1980). *Meditation: Self-Regulation Strategy & Altered States of Consciousness.* (New York: Aldine), p. 14.

6. K. Guentert (1982). Twenty-four old/new ways to pray. *U.S. Catholic,* 12, pp. 17-24.

7. H. Benson & M. Klipper (1975). *The Relaxation Response.* (New York: Avon Books.)

8. L. LeShan (1974). *How to Meditate: A Guide to Self-Discovery.* (Boston: Little, Brown, & Co.)

CHAPTER 13

1. D. Shapiro, et al. (Eds.) (1971-1981). *Biofeedback and Behavioral Medicine: Therapeutic Applications and Experimental Foundations.* (New York: Aldine.)

2. T. Budzynsky (1978). Biofeedback in the treatment of muscle contraction (tension) headache. Task force report of the Biofeedback Society of America, *Biofeedback and Self-Regulation,* 3, pp. 409-434.

3. R. Surwit (1982). Biofeedback treatment of Raynaud's Syndrome in peripheral vascular disease. *Journal of Consulting and Clinical Psychology,* December, pp. 922-932.

4. E. Green, A. Green & P. Norris (1980). Self-regulation of training of hypertension: An experimental method for restoring or maintaining normal blood pressure. *Primary Cardiology,* 6.

5. W. Dember (1960). *The Psychology of Perception.* (New York: Holt, Rinehart, & Winston.)

CHAPTER 14

1. J. Basmajian, (Ed.) (1983). *Biofeedback: Principles and Practice for Clinicians (3rd ed.).* (Baltimore: Williams & Wilkins.)

2. Ibid.

3. D. Williamson & E. Blanchard (1979). Heart rate and blood pressure biofeedback: a review of the recent experimental literature. *Biofeedback and Self-Regulation,* 4(1), pp. 1-34.

4. J. Lubar (1983). EEG biofeedback and neurological applications. In Basmajian, J. (Ed.) (1983). *Biofeedback: Principles and Practice for Clinicians (3rd ed.).* (Baltimore: Williams and Wilkins.)

CHAPTER 15

1. J. Curtis & R. Detert (1985). *Learn To Relax: A 14-Day Program.* (La Crosse: Coulee Press), pp. 87-88.

2. J. Curtis & R. Detert (1981). *How To Relax: A Holistic Approach to Stress Management.* (Palo Alto: Mayfield), p. 156.

3. Ibid., pp. 156-168.

4. J. Curtis & R. Detert (1985), p. 90.

5. C. F. Strobel. Quieting Reflex: A Choice For Adults. Audio Cassettes, Clinician's and Self-Instruction Manuals. QR Institute, 119 Forest Dr., Wethersfield, CN. 06109.

6. M. Edwards (1981). Stress Management Education. In R. Russell (Ed.), *Education in the 80's: Health Education.* (Washington: National Education Association.)

CHAPTER 16

1. R. Rohey & A. Raizner (1983). The cold pressor test in evaluating cardiovascular disease. *Practical Cardiology,* 9(12), pp. 123-131.

2. L. Derogatis, R. Lipman & L. Covi (1973). The SCL-90: An outpatient psychiatric rating scale. *Psychopharmacological Bulletin,* 9, pp. 13-28.

3. C. Speilberger, R. Gorsuch & R. Lushene (1970). *State-Trait Anxiety Manual.* (Palo Alto: Consulting Psychologist Press.)

4. A. Beck, et al. (1961). An inventory for measuring depression. *Archives of General Psychiatry,* 4, p. 561.

5. T. Holmes & R. Rahe (1967). The social readjustment rating scale. *Journal of Psychosomatic Research,* 11, pp. 213-218.

6. M. Friedman & R. Rosenman (1974). *Type A Behavior and Your Heart.* (New York: Knopf.)

7. R. Rosenman, et al. (1964). A predictive study of coronary heart disease. *Journal of the American Medical Association,* 189, p. 15.

8. R. Rosenman, et al. (1975). Coronary heart disease in the western collaborative group study: Final follow up experience of 8 1/2 years. *Journal of the American Medical Association,* 233, pp. 872-877.

9. Ibid.

10. Ibid.

11. Ibid.

12. Public Health Service (1977). A concurrent validational study of the NCHS general well-being schedule (DHEW Publication # HRA78-1347). *Vital & Health Statistics,* (Series 2-Number 73. Washington, D.C.: U.S. Government Printing Office.)

13. Ibid.

14. IOX Assessment Associates (1983). *An Evaluation Handbook for Health Education Programs in Stress Management,* (Contract No. 200-81-0622). Center for Health Promotion and Education, Centers for Disease Control.

CHAPTER 17

1. M. Friedman & R. Rosemnan (1974). *Type A Behavior and Your Heart.* (New York: Knopf.)

2. D. Burns (1980). *Feeling Good: The New Mood Therapy.* (New York: Signet.)

3. M. Mahoney & C. Thorensen (1974). *Self-Control: Power to the Person.* (Monterey, CA: Brooks/Cole.)

4. D. Watson & R. Tharp (1981). *Self-Directed Behavior: Self-Modification for Personal Adjustment,(3rd ed.).* (Monterey, CA: Brooks/Cole.)

5. D. Burns (1980).

6. A. Ellis & R. Harper (1979). *A New Guide to Rational Living.* (Hollywood, CA: Wilshire Book Co.)

CHAPTER 20

1. Audio Visual Division/3M (1984). *How to Present More Effectively - and With More Favorable Responses from More People in Less Time.* (St. Paul: 3M Corporation.)

2. J. Curtis & R. Detert (1981). *How To Relax: A Holistic Approach to Stress Managment.* (Palo Alto: Mayfield), pp. 177-178.

3. R. Wyman (1957). *The Option Is Ours.* (Holyoke, Massachusetts: Tecnifax Corporation), p. 2.

4. J. Kemp (1975). *Planning and Producing Audiovisual Materials.* (New York: Thomas Y. Crowell), pp. 196-199.

5. Audio Visual Division/3M (1984).

6. J. Brown, R. Lewis & F. Harcleroad (1973). *AV Instruction: Technology, Media and Methods.* (New York: McGraw-Hill Book Company), p. 136.

7. Audio Visual Division/3M (1984).

8. J. Bullard & C. Mether (1984). *Audiovisual Fundamentals.* (Dubuque, Iowa: William C. Brown Co.Publishers), pp. 128-129.

9. C. Rood (1985). *The Making of a Good Visual.* (La Crosse: Mimeographed handout), p. 1.

10. J. Brown, R. Lewis & F. Harcleroad (1973). pp. 192-194.

INDEX

SUPPORTIVE TEACHING SUPPLIES

The following stress management materials are available from:
Coulee Press and Distributing
P.O. Box 1744
La Crosse, Wisconsin 54602-1744

The Stress Management Card

The stress management card is a simple, easy-to-use, inexpensive biofeedback device based on the principle that tension causes constriction of the blood vessels and, thus, cold hands. As a person relaxes, the blood vessels on the surface of the extremities dialate thus warming the hands and increasing the temperature. The Stress Management Card pictured below is a four-color card with temperature-sensitive liquid-crystal paper that responds to changing temperature by changing color. The card can be used by itself with the two stress management techniques on the back or with the coordinated materials. (i.e. *The Learn To Relax: A 14-Day Program* book and cassette tape).

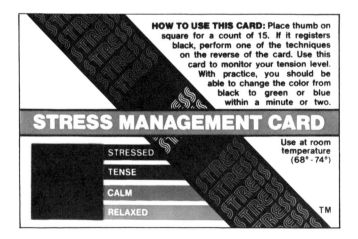

How to Use The Card

To monitor your level of tension and/or relaxation, place your thumb lightly on the black square for approximately fifteen seconds. Then check the color directly under the thumb.

Black. . . . . Stressed
Red/Brown . . . . Tense
Green . . . . Calm
Blue. . . . . Relaxed

Use The Card To Check Your Tension Level

Periodically throughout the day, check your level of tension with the biofeedback card. If the card reads black or red, do a relaxation technique or an instant relaxation technique and, if you've mastered the skills, the card will change to green or blue.

Use The Card To Check Your Effectiveness At Relaxing

1.   Check your level of tension prior to taking time to relax.
2.   Perform selected relaxation techniques.
3.   Check your level of relaxation after you have performed the techniques. With practice, most people can turn the card from black to blue in one to five minutes if they have practiced the techniques on a regular basis.

How To Order The Card

The durable, credit card-size Stress Management Card fits easily into a purse or wallet so that it is with you when you need it. The card works well in a class setting because it provides immediate feedback to the participants that the techniques are working when they relax and change the color.

1 card $3.95
2 - 3 . . . . 2.95
4 - 9 . . . . 2.50
10 - 19 . . . . 2.25
20 - 29 . . . . 2.00
30 - 49 . . . . 1.75
50 - 100 . . . . 1.60
    Discounts available at higher amounts.

Books

Learn To Relax: A 14-Day Program by John D. Curtis, Ph. D., and Richard A. Detert. Second edition. Coulee Press. 112 pages, 18 photographs, 1985.

A simple, easy-to-follow book that teaches the basics of relaxation. The book includes classroom-tested relaxation exercises, a fourteen-day log, motivational techniques, questions and answers, and a new chapter on instant relaxation techniques. The authors have over 19 years of experience between them teaching relaxation classes to students, educators, medical professionals, athletes, prison inmates, law enforcement agencies, and to people in business and industry. **$4.95**

How To Relax: A Holistic Approach to Stress Management by John D. Curtis, Ph. D., and Richard A. Detert. Mayfield Publishing Co. 222 pages, illustrated, 1981.

A detailed, self-care stress management book for people who want to do more than just cope with stress. This book includes more than 30 relaxation and sensory awareness exercises. Chapters on time management, the mind, communication skills, practical relaxation skills and the role of nutrition and exercise are included. This book is used in stress management and relaxation classes throughout the United States and in six foreign countries. **$12.95**

Teaching Stress Management and Relaxation Skills: An Instructor's Guide by John D. Curtis, Ph. D., Richard A. Detert, Ph. D., Jay Schindler, Ph.D., and Kip Zirkel, Ph.D. Coulee Press, 275 pages, 15 photographs, illustrated, index, 1985.

The most comprehensive book on teaching stress management available today. Written by professionals with combined experience of almost 40 years in teaching stress management, biofeedback and related courses. Twenty chapters cover all aspects of stress management. The book emphasizes Instructional Pointers which are detailed suggestions for improving classes that normally only come from years of experience. The foreword was written by Meyer Friedman, M. D. of Type A Behavior fame. This book is destined to become the bible of stress management **$26.50**

Cassette

The Learn To Relax cassette tape contains the four basic relaxation techniques from the book, *Learn To Relax: A 14-Day Program*. The cassette can be used to lead you into a deeply relaxed state. Each exercise is followed by six to ten minutes of silence to allow adequate time to relax. **$8.95**

The Stress Management Kit

Includes:

Learn To Relax: A 14-Day Program book
Learn to Relax: A 14-Day Program cassette
Stress Management Card

This is the only complete stress management kit available today. The combination of the book that describes and teaches the relaxation techniques, the cassette that leads you through the techniques, and the stress management card that monitors your success at relaxation makes this unique kit in stress management
. . . . **$14.95**

Special Packages

The following special packages are available to instructors of stress management programs and to institutions to help make instructor training and stress management classes more rewarding.

The Instructor's Package includes:

Teaching Stress Management and Relaxation Skills: An Instructor's Guide ($26.50).
Learn To Relax: A 14-Day Program ($4.95).
The *Learn To Relax* Cassette Tape ($8.95).
Two Stress Management Cards ($7.90).
How To Relax: A Holistic Approach to Stress Management ($12.95).

A $61. 25 value if items were purchased separately . . . *Save* when you buy the package for **$54.95**

The Patient Education Package includes:

3 Stress Management Kits. A $44.85 value for **$39.95**

The Stress Management Class Package includes:

10 *Learn To Relax* Books and 10 Stress Management Cards. A $69.50 value for only **$59.95**

About The Authors

John D. Curtis, Ph.D.

John D. Curtis, Ph.D., is a professor in the Department of Health Education at the University of Wisconsin-La Crosse and the founder and director of the UW-La Crosse Stress Management Institute which trains health care providers to teach stress management classes. He has done extensive lecturing and conducting of workshops and inservices in the area of stress management and relaxation techniques with businesses, hospitals, educators, law enforcement personnel, health care professionals, and social workers throughout the United States and Canada. Dr. Curtis has served as a relaxation consultant to the U.S. Olympic and National Ski Jumping Teams. He is also co-author of seven health books including *How To Relax: A Holistic Approach to Stress Management* and *Learn To Relax: A 14-Day Program*.

Richard A. Detert, Ph.D.

Richard A. Detert, Ph.D., received his doctorate in health education from Southern Illinois University, Carbondale. He is an assistant professor in the Department of Health Education at the University of Wisconsin-La Crosse and a faculty member of the UW-La Crosse Stress Management Institute. Dr. Detert has conducted stress management workshops throughout the Midwest for businesses, educators, students, lay persons, athletes, and prison inmates. He is co-author of *How To Relax: A Holistic Approach to Stress Management* and *Learn To Relax: A 14-Day Program*.

Jay V. Schindler, Ph.D.

Jay V. Schindler, Ph.D., received his M.S. in Biology and Ph.D. in Health and Safety Education from the University of Illinois. He is an associate professor in the Department of Health Education at the University of Wisconsin-La Crosse.

Dr. Schindler has taught courses in biofeedback and self-regulation for the past three years, and has provided teacher inservices, workshops, and community presentations on the topics of stress management, biofeedback, and ameliorating stress-induced disorders.

Kip Zirkel, Ph.D.

Kip Zirkel, Ph.D., received his B.A. in psychology from the University of Texas, and his Ph.D. in counseling psychology from Ohio State University. He is presently director of the Biofeedback Clinic of the University of Wisconsin-La Crosse and has been engaged in biofeedback and stress management training for ten years. Dr. Zirkel has authored articles in the field of biofeedback and has conducted many workshops and training sessions in biofeedback and stress management.